D0810242

Pastoral Care and Psychotherapy

Pastoral Care and Psychotherapy

A Study in Cooperation Between
Physician and Pastor

BY PEDER OLSEN

TRANSLATED BY HERMAN E. JORGENSEN

Augsburg Publishing House
Minneapolis 15, Minnesota

This volume is a translation of the Norwegian book *Sjele-sorg og Psykoterapi—Samarbeid mellom lege og prest,* published in 1959 by Lutherstiftelsen, Oslo, Norway

Translator's Preface

This book, written by an experienced chaplain at the Lovisen-berg Deaconess Hospital in Oslo, Norway, deals largely with spiritual guidance given hospital patients and other persons in need of help for bodily ailments and for psychic and spiritual distress. This spiritual guidance is in the native language of the author called *Sjelesorg* (akin to German *Seelsorge*), which literally means *soul care*. I am aware that there is some division of opinion in our country as to the most fortunate designation for such spiritual guidance as this book deals with, and of the circumstance that the preponderant choice of terminology seems here to be *pastoral care*.

However, I have in my translation often made use of the term *soul care* for the following reasons:

In the first place, because it is the designation used by the author, and because his entire presentation places the emphasis on the fact that the spiritual guidance discussed is for the *soul* of the individual involved, and only secondarily on the fact that guidance usually is given by a pastor. (I add, in passing, that I do not overlook the fact that the term pastor in this connection is used rather in its original sense of shepherd than as a synonym for clergyman.)

In the second place, because I find myself in hearty accord with the emphasis laid by the author. The most important thing in giving spiritual guidance is that the *soul* of the one seeking help is given spiritual food. While the person of the one giving the guidance is important, it in no way outranks the importance of the needy soul in its outreach for help.

I desire to call attention to the fact that in my translation I have also used the term pastoral care, first, to avoid a too frequent use of the term soul care, secondly, to stress the importance of the person administering the care of souls whenever the author does that very thing.

Lastly, I want to admit that I have purposely avoided the use of the same designation every time the author uses the term *sjelesørger* for the one giving soul care. The reason is, primarily, that the English has no exact equivalent, and, in the second place, to avoid monotony of expression. I have sometimes used the term pastor, or some related expression; at other times I have made use of soul counselor (analogously with the designation youth counselor, which lately has appeared in our congregational life).

HERMAN E. JORGENSEN

Minneapolis, January, 1961

Author's Preface

In recent years the question about border lines between soul care and psychotherapy has awakened a lively interest as a field for thoroughgoing research, especially among psychotherapists. But also churchmen have become aware of the importance of such a study. The relation between soul care and psychotherapy is recognized to be a subject, not only of theoretical interest, but also of the greatest possible importance to physician and clergyman alike in order that both, in the special work of each as well as in their cooperation, may be enabled to give their fellow men the best and most efficient help.

But also other professional groups encounter in their work problems closely related to soul care and to psychotherapy. As such may be mentioned psychologists, nurses, social workers, educators, lawyers, etc.

If we in our day are to be enabled to give our fellow men thorough assistance, all forces working for the betterment of mankind must unite in positive cooperation, preferably in a teamwork of organic concurrence. A person in distress is in need not only of medical and psychiatric, physiologic, and social help, but also of sound assistance in solving his ethico-religious problems.

This book seeks to show that soul care has its necessary function in this cooperative effort to assist men in need, since soul care calls attention to and tries to meet a need common to all men. It is meant also as a challenge to the Church to become increasingly aware of its curative responsibility. For precisely in the field of soul care lies its greatest possibility for reaching men for the express purpose of giving them the help they need, and for which they often long, consciously or unconsciously.

I wish to add that this book is the result of a close cooperation carried on for years by physicians and pastors in our city; and that it is published in the hope that it may be an encouragement and a help, also elsewhere, for those interested in and working with the problems which it discusses.

PEDER OLSEN

Oslo, August, 1959

Contents

Pastoral Care and
Psychotherapy

Chapter I

Is Pastoral Care Needed Today?

That pastoral care is greatly needed today may be uniformly asserted by all who practice it. An ever-increasing number of persons turn to their pastors for counsel and help, and many pastors have as many calls for such help as they can possibly answer. Indeed, there are pastors whose appointment schedule for counseling of this kind is filled for quite some time ahead, doubtless to their great joy. People have discovered afresh that one of the main functions of clergymen is to serve as spiritual guides and counselors. But, even so, only a few of the many who need, desire, and look for help through soul care, have this need actually met.

Furthermore, the spiritual need is even greater than has been stated above, as we may safely take into account the presence of a latent ethico-religious need with practically all men. This need may become conscious and actual before one realizes it. That is a part of the surprises, inconsequences, and irrationalities abounding in actual life. The Bible tells us that the Holy Spirit is the cause of this: "The wind blows where it wills, and you hear the sound of it, but you do not know whence it comes or whither it goes; so it is with every one who is born of the Spirit" (John 3:8).

Experience has shown that where access to soul care is provided, and where the possibilities for contact are tactfully, discreetly, and patiently made use of, there the spiritual need is awakened with an attendant increase of requests for counsel.

Thus the situation in the matter of soul care today is a potent challenge to the Church. The question arises whether this challenge is met as it ought. There is no exaggeration in the assertion that personal soul care is one of the most effective means, fraught with the greatest possibilities, toward giving men of today access to that salvation and succor which God has given his Church to administer.

Who else, indeed, than the pastors should participate in the discharge of the Church's clear responsibility of caring for souls? A clergyman is, in very deed, called to be a *pastor* (shepherd), always ready to extend help to those who need soul care.

It is, of course, true that various views regarding the real nature of soul care exist, both among those who endeavor to give it and among those who need it. Often these views may be vague and confused, a condition which naturally works harm. Or they may be so circumscribed or lacking in understanding as to limit the usefulness of the soul care in question.

There are several callings in which there is a special demand for soul care, both of a practical and of a theoretical nature. Among these are: pastors and other theologically trained men, physicians, nurses, psychologists, social workers, lawyers, teachers, and other pedagogues. But in this book we purpose to discuss mainly some of the most common problems occurring in the cooperative efforts of *physicians and pastors,* and to concentrate on the relation between soul care and psychotherapy.

It has been demonstrated by experience that soul care and psychotherapy have much in common. Some of the same problems are encountered also within other callings.

Many of those who seek counsel with pastors receive help, not only religiously, but often also in other respects. This may be help in adjusting conflicts in marriage and other family relations, e.g., in sexual matters; or help toward resolving economic or social difficulties; or help in bringing relief or restoration of health to those who are ill. Soul care may change a person's entire outlook on life.

Under such circumstances it is not strange that men turn to pastors for help. This occurs most often when sickness invades the home. Then pastoral care is sought, not primarily to obtain spiritual help, but to get help toward healing of the body.

There is, then, in evidence a tendency toward viewing soul care chiefly as a curative measure. And often it gets to be something in the line of a last resort. Not infrequently the remark is heard, "I have tried everything, in vain. Now nothing is left but to try prayer." If the person concerned is not in the habit of praying, he is usually glad, in that mood, to turn to those who are. But even pastors must guard against dangers in such situations.

When a pastor succeeds in being of help to a fellow man, not only in the matter of spiritual release, but also of regaining bodily health, the thought may readily intrude itself that soul care is so closely related to healing that it should be employed more effectively, more according to a conscious plan. He is tempted to ask whether soul care is not also psychotherapy. And ought he not make use of all the means and methods available to render soul care more effectual in the effort to bring about psychic soundness and bodily healing?

In the exercise of this office the pastor will meet many who are afflicted with psychic weaknesses and nervous sufferings. Ought he at once to turn these over to a neurologist, a psychiatrist, or a psychotherapist? Or should he as a pastor inform and equip himself so as to endeavor to help and heal the nervously afflicted who come to him seeking pastoral care?

Thus we see that the soul counselor and the psychotherapist operate in close proximity, in the same field.

But also physicians often come in contact with the problems of soul care. Most of those who seek a physician's help come because of some physical or psychic ailment. Experience has amply demonstrated that psychosomatic symptoms are not always caused by organic ailments. Very often the cause is to be sought elsewhere, e.g., in the sufferer's own surroundings, or in his social *milieu,* his inter-personal plane; or it may have connection with spiritual factors or with religio-ethical conditions. A physician encountering these problems in his practice may deal with them in various ways. He may, for instance, refuse to deal with them, either on the plea that they belong outside of his province, or that he lacks competence in the matter, and in consequence refer the patient elsewhere. But there are many physicians who feel that they cannot evade the issue, feeling assured that the adjustment of the ethico-religious conflict may be of importance for obtaining psychic well-being and physical cure. If the patient gets adequate spiritual help, the result may have a positive effect on his state of health. Experience has here shown that many patients have been definitely helped through the spiritual guidance given by the physician.

In such situations the question arises for the physician whether to give his patients soul care or not. And then it is inescapable that he either refers to or directly uses the means of soul care if his patient is to be helped out of his ethico-religious need. In many instances the physician himself then must give religious counsel and guidance.

Hence, also seen from the physician's point of view, it is apparent that there is a relationship between soul care and psychotherapy. But also other questions press for an answer in the handling of this problem.

For instance: May soul care and psychotherapy be combined? Must psychotherapy also be soul care in order to achieve the best possible results in dealing with patients? Has the psychotherapist the necessary professional training and other requisite qualifications for giving soul care? Or, are these two entirely different fields of endeavor, without mutual relationship?

It is thus seen that it is of special importance to gain a clear conception of the relationship between the two. Such a clarification has not only a theoretical significance, but it is of decisive importance both for pastors and for physicians in their respective labors. And such clarification will, eventually, benefit both the sick and the well.

If we are to arrive at a clear answer to the questions raised it is of primary importance that we get a clear conception of what we mean in our usage of the terms psychotherapy and soul care.

Chapter II

What Is
Psychotherapy?

The word itself does not mean much to the average reader. Psychotherapy is derived from the Greek term *therapeia psychés,* which means treatment of the soul life. Hence, soul care and psychotherapy have this in common that they deal with the soul, the word "soul" being a part of each term. Conceptually considered it would thus seem that soul care stresses the *care* of the "soul," while psychotherapy emphasizes the *treatment* of the "soul."

But this linguistic differentiation really gives little essential information. The decisive criterion is the meaning which usage through the years has attached to the words. Each one is the exponent of a definite sphere of action, with its own objectives, its own particular means and methods of procedure.

In order to arrive at an understanding of what psychotherapy and soul care have in common and of what distinguishes one from the other, we must have a clear perception of what is meant by psychotherapy and of what soul care means. A presentation of the history of each might here be in order, interesting as well as useful, but the compass of our study forbids it. The interest would particularly be on the side of psychotherapy, as it is medical science's oldest therapeutic means and played a prominent role even in antiquity. History tells us that psychotherapy was once marked by sorcery, magic, superstition—magnetism—but also that it has fought its way, through the most diversified phases, up to sober, scientific methods of treatment.

However, it is not easy to say definitely what psychotherapy is, and even more difficult to define it exactly. Contrariwise, it is possible to say something about that which *characterizes* psychotherapy and what makes it a separate and distinctive curative treatment.

In his textbook on clinical psychiatry Professor Gabriel Langfeldt, M.D., says: "Psychotherapy is a collective designation for all general and individual methods of treatment having as their aim, by psychic means, to prevent, ameliorate, and eventually to cure psychic anomalies, warped developments, and ills of the mind.

"As we shall later note, that which acts in an immediate way in several of these methods is of a suggestive and autosuggestive nature, a circumstance which explains that quacks, even without the least qualifications for understanding human ills of a psychic nature, fairly often may have an immediate success with their treatments, even where a psychotherapeutic treatment done by a trained physician may have failed. But developments have increasingly brought it about that psychotherapy has become the special province of physicians specially trained in that art, even though some of the psychotherapeutic methods may also be employed by physicians in general practice and also by others called on to assist men in mental conflicts and psychic need."

Psychotherapy has developed a number of different methods having their own methodology and technique, as well as their own special scope of indications.

Although there are many different ways of practicing psychotherapy, these methods nevertheless have this in common that they all are meant to be a *treatment* of psychic life. This treatment, like all curative treatment, must be undertaken on a logical, rational basis, without taking account of religious ideas. Treatment of psychic conditions, even as treatment of the body, has a wholly empiric foundation. It must be based on the observations and experiments of human psychic behavior under both normal and abnormal conditions, combined with modern concepts of the psychic structure: subconsciousness, psychic reflexes, repressions, etc.

The goal of psychotherapy is healing of the sick psychic life. It aims at psychic health and release, and it creates the best possible conditions for the sound functioning of the *psyche* according to the laws and powers of the *psyche*. The psychotherapeutic constellation is named: sick—sound, and this situation arises in the contacts between patient and physician.

Chapter III

What Is
Pastoral Care?

While psychotherapy belongs to medical science, soul care is classified under theology. It is a distinct part of that division of the science of theology known as practical theology. Soul care—pastoral theology—is a distinct, scientific branch of theology, with characteristics of its own, having a long and honorable history and valuable, highly esteemed traditions.

In the course of centuries various traditions, each one typical of the epoch concerned, of denominational characteristics, and of spiritual and cultural currents, have developed. In the early days of Christianity the main stress was laid on the individual Christian's responsibility toward his own soul as well as towards others. (See 1 Tim. 5:8.) And even though no separate pastoral office distinctly charged with soul care can be traced, it is evident that the spiritual leaders of the time had such a special responsibility. Suffice it to mention the charge of Jesus to Peter: "Feed my lambs" and "Feed my sheep"; or such passages as Acts 20:18-38, and the admonitions in the Pastoral Epistles to those having a special service in the churches.

In the Early Church soul care was attached to the several

ecclesiastical offices: bishops *(episkopoi)*, elders *(presbyteroi)*, deacons, and deaconesses *(diakonoi)*, and became increasingly institutionalized, especially when practiced in connection with private confession and institutions of penance.

During the Middle Ages the Roman Catholic Church put its special imprint also on the giving of soul care. The Church became *the* institution of salvation *("Extra ecclesia nulla salus")* taking over the responsibility for man's salvation, but on the condition that the individual maintain the right relation to the Church, receive her spiritual benefits, and obey her teachings and ordinances. The aim and office of administering soul care was to effectuate this salvation of the Church to the individual, and this took place through the priestly function, specifically in the *confessional*. Thus the priest's office became of paramount importance. Gregory the Great designated the giving of soul care as "the holy office of guidance." And the priest was regarded as the commander of souls *(rector animarum)*. This pronounced regimentation of souls was emphasized through church discipline carried out through various kinds and degrees of punishments and penances.

Roman Catholic soul care has also developed a thorough, detailed casuistry designed to help the priest in giving answers, help, and counsel on behalf of the Church.

The Reformation brought about a new concept of soul care. Through Luther's personal experience the biblical truth regarding justification by faith was revived; it was recognized that man is saved through faith in Jesus Christ. In consequence the evangelical idea of soul care takes exception to the idea of soul regimentation and gives the souls themselves the possibility and the power to make, voluntarily, the right choice and the right action. Thus, soul care is not to employ compulsion and coercive means, but only the persuasive power of the Word of God. While the Reformed churches, guided by Calvin and Zwingli, largely follow the course of Luther, this difference may be noted, that they make more use of the Law than of the Gospel, for which reason outward church discipline plays a larger part in them than in the Lutheran Church.

Space forbids a more extensive historical survey. Those interested in further study along this line are referred to a modest bibliography at the close of this book. I desire only in passing to mention that Christian soul care has a great heritage to maintain and rich sources to consult.

The pastoral-theologic literature from ancient times up to the present is both extensive and valuable, and it will pay richly to study it. While perusing these writings the reader will often have occasion to marvel at the intelligence, wisdom, and pastoral insight here displayed. Mention should also be made of the confessions of various denominations, as they bear evidence of awareness of pastoral responsibility. Likewise the wealth of worth-while devotional literature, as well as of hymnology. These treasures, having sprung from the numberless experiences occurring in religious life, are rich sources of inspiration in practically all situations which the pastor meets, a veritable gold mine for one who cares to explore it. It is reported that a Swedish bishop (Herman Rundgren) was wont to spend several days together with his candidates for ordination impressing upon them the importance of acquainting themselves with the classics of devotional literature, giving not only a brief survey, but a thorough induction into the subject. "Note carefully what this book says," he would say. "Pay attention to the exact wording, and ponder why it is so expressed. Then you need not be embarrassed at a remark like this one: 'The pastor will doubtless recall what Johann Arndt says in such and such a chapter.'"

What has so far been said serves to place soul care in its true perspective. We have noted that soul care is an independent and distinctive institution belonging to the Church, and that it is characterized by its aim, its definite objective, and its specific means.

It is really God himself who is the transactor in soul care. He is the initiative and acting force in his dealings with souls, meant for all. But he transacts his care of souls through human agents. As God has in this relationship made himself dependent on human aid, soul care is accordingly both divine and human. The rule is: No preaching without a preacher; no baptism without a baptizer; no Eucharist without one who administers and distributes the gifts of God's grace; etc.

From the point of view of soul care the relation to God is the decisive matter. Man is created by God and for communion with God; man's greatest adversity and deepest misery is that he has broken away from God and is living outside communion with him. The purpose of soul care is to lead men back to God. When men are brought into the right relationship with God they are also brought into the right relationship with themselves, with their fellow men, and with the world. It is thus not *our* will that soul care seeks to promote, but the will of God. And what the will of God is, is clearly set forth in the Bible: "This is good, and it is acceptable in the sight of God our Savior, *who desires all men to be saved* and to come to the knowledge of the truth" (1 Tim. 2:3-4).

The aim of soul care is to realize God's will with us and in us; and his will is our salvation, eternal salvation. Besides this everything else dwindles into insignificance.

"For what does it profit a man, to gain the whole world and forfeit his life? For what can a man give in return for his life?" Jesus asks in Mark 8:36-37. Jesus here takes cognizance of the soul's absolute and eternal welfare. Thus, the most important thing for soul care is the soul's salvation. The Bible tells us that salvation is not merely a goal and a desire of God for us, but it is something which he himself has made possible for us through Jesus Christ. "And there is salvation in no one else, for there is no other name under heaven given among men by which we must be saved" (Acts 4:12).

Accordingly the essence of soul care is leading men to Christ, to him who himself is the way, the truth, and the life. It may also be stated thus: to lead Christ to the individual.

Of paramount interest to the administrator of soul care is that the will of God is accomplished with and in a person. From this point of view it may be said that "soul care is everything that you do for a person in order that God may have his will with him" (as stated by Bishop Smemo of Oslo in a recent lecture). But if God's will is to be attained toward a man, then he must *come to the knowledge of the truth.*"

This acknowledgment of truth is to be effectuated by soul care. For unto the realization of this end God has placed at the disposal of the dispenser of soul care certain means and methods of action, entrusted by him to his Church on earth: the Bible, preaching, teaching, witnessing, the Sacraments, prayer, the Communion of Saints, the private confessional. All of these means may be summarized in the term: the Word of God, when understood in its widest sense, with varying forms of expression.

And soul care is to function as the servant of the Word, *minister verbi divini.* Therefore do preaching and soul care belong together; they are inseparable, since soul care is an organic part of preaching, having as its function to *proclaim the Gospel and to give the answer and succor of the Word of God to the individual in his concrete and factual situations.*

But true preaching must also be soul care, as all preaching should be impelled by loving concern for one's fellow men. Without this concern preaching gets to be empty, soulless words, ineffectual utterance of comfort and counsel, bearing the stamp only of technique, routine, and outward considerations. Preachers are to be servants of Jesus Christ, instruments for the transforming of the love and spirit of God to their fellow men. Results are not always dependent on what we say and do; of greater importance is what we *are*. For soul care *may*, indeed, be given without words, only through what we are. The decisive thing for obtaining results in soul care is the *spirit*—the atmosphere—pervading it. "Have this mind among yourselves, which you have in Christ Jesus" (Phil. 2:5)

But having the mind which was in Christ means having the same concern for men as he had. In his soul care, concern for men's bodily, physical need was an integral part. He healed the sick, fed the hungry, cast out evil spirits, gave peace and security and light to fear-ridden, depressed men. The general impression of the Christ of the Gospels is that he helped men in *all* kinds of need. This impression is taken for granted as we are wont to think of Christ as a wholly exceptional being, but we forget too readily the very essential truth that the concern of Jesus for man's welfare is something meant to be a constant, living reality in the Church. And what is implied in this statement? This, that concern for bodily, physical human need is legitimate soul care. The Bible gives us the right to say this in even stronger words: That soul care which in actual practice is unaware of its responsibility for suffering humanity, in both physical and psychic need, has failed in its mission. Remember such solemn words as these: "But if anyone . . . sees his brother in need, yet closes his heart against him, how does God's love abide in him?" (1 John 3:17.)

Or let us call to mind the severe judgment pronounced on those who omit assistance to the sick, the poor, the imprisoned, the hungry and thirsty, etc. "As you did it not to one of the least of these, you did it not to me" (Matt. 25:45). Jesus does more than lay great stress on this concern; he makes it evident that it is part and parcel of his Messianic call and mission. It was actually a proof that he was the one he declared himself to be. (Matt. 11:2-6.)

For this reason he gave his disciples the same might and dominion over sickness and death. He gave them *exousia,* i.e., "power and authority over all demons and to cure diseases" at the same time as "he sent them out to preach the kingdom of God" (Luke 9:1-2). And this power and will to help were not given only to the twelve, but to the Church, as an enduring possession.

This kind of soul care was administered in the New Testament churches; and church history records that the same practice was in evidence throughout the first three centuries.

It is true that this concept of soul care was later forced into retreat by a rather one-sided spiritualized view, which has stressed spiritual healing to the virtual exclusion of concern for the physical and psychic need, a development which has wrought injury to the sick and suffering, and which constitutes a breach of the command of him who is both the author and the finisher of soul care.

Consequently, if we are to regain a truly biblical view of soul care, concern for man's bodily and psychic needs must be regarded, not merely as a legitimate part of soul care, but as an absolute consequence and sequence of loyalty to Christ.

From ancient times we have a beautiful designation for soul care, one that covers all the points so far named: *cura animarum*. It expresses primarily concern for souls, for their salvation, but the *cura,* i.e., cure, medical treatment, covers also care of the sick, those in need of healing.

Therefore, in true soul care efforts should be made to integrate the healing powers of all biblical means in the administration of pastoral care.

Chapter IV

Relationships

In the course of time the relation between soul care and psychotherapy has become increasingly actual, and has also been eagerly discussed and studied. Throughout the world attempts are being made at clarifying the points of contact which the two fields have in common. This development has, doubtless, a distinct relation to the mutual interest, understanding, respect, and positive evaluation now existing between physicians and pastors, a circumstance which in turn has brought about a greater and more fruitful cooperation between psychotherapists and those in charge of soul care.

Clergymen have gained a clearer perception of the useful assistance to be derived from psychotherapy in general and of its use in soul care in particular. And physicians have discovered "the soul" and the importance of spiritual values and factors, such as conscience, view of life, faith, and prayer, recognizing the part which these play in personality, in psychic well-being, and in bodily health.

The many meetings, conferences, gatherings, and congresses now arranged in various countries by physicians and clergymen prove that the two professional groups have, in a new way, come within speaking distance of each other.

They endeavor to understand each other's field of labor and to arrive at a correct and fruitful relationship between pastors and psychotherapists.

The solution of these problems has been attempted in several ways, but we shall mention only two such attempts in order to clarify the situation. These two ways of procedure are most likely the farthest apart, but they are symptomatic of what is peculiar to the time and the situation.

That which characterizes one of these lines of thought is a *one-sided stress on the similarity between soul care and psychotherapy; it represents a view which practically places an equality mark between the two.*

A typical representative of this view is Dr. Poul Bjerre of Sweden, who in 1940 founded the Institute for Medical Psychology and Psychotherapy. In 1942 this institute published a book entitled *Själavård–Själsvård*. By the term *själavård* is here meant an enlarged soul care—"one able to meet the great curative need of the innumerable individuals having psychic ailments in the various situations and relations of life"; *själsvård* as here used is another expression for psychotherapy. Thus, instead of differentiating between soul care and psychotherapy Dr. Bjerre equates them.

Dr. Bjerre's motive in so doing is doubtless good. He wishes to help the sufferers on the horizontal plane. In his book he thus tells a moving story of a countrywoman who was cured of a neurosis. In his psychotherapeutic conversations with her he also dealt with her religious problems. But when Dr. Bjerre later, in his comments on the case, interprets religious ideas and spiritual values one can hardly help feeling dubious, as he interprets them in his own special way and gives imputations to her expressions quite otherwise than she doubtless meant them.

When the patient spoke of sin and guilt, for which she was in need of God's forgiveness, he maintains that "guilt emotions in connection with marriage relations have nothing to do with the eternal laws of God, but are human inventions; or, in more scientific language, they are the results of construed moral fictions."

At the patient's mention of the help received through faith in Jesus Dr. Bjerre's reaction is that her religious terminology is wholly insignificant; he takes into account only immanent forces as operative in the healing process, leaving no room for transcendent forces. For the patient herself both her spiritual life and the help which she received were evidently theocentrically orientated, while for Dr. Bjerre the cure had entirely anthropocentric orientation.

He also attributes to Christian concepts a wholly different import than they really have; he tries, in fact, to translate Christian terms into psychotherapeutic phraseology. Thus, faith in Christ gets to be a designation for renewal of the *psyche;* grace a synonym for the healing power of nature; prayer, contemplation; salvation, the humanization of the person. Everything gets to be the work of man, not of God.

The cause of this confusion of concepts and terms is found in the circumstance that soul care and psychotherapy are confounded—*själavård* (soul care) has become *själsvård* (psychotherapy). This confusion may easily get to have dangerous consequences: yielding to the temptation of over-looking and ignoring absolute values and spiritual factors with their effect on personality.

The obliteration of boundaries between soul care and psychotherapy will lead to a development which is bound to render the use of both soul care and psychotherapy trivial, even futile, with the greatest harm done to soul care, which in this way will lose its distinctiveness and its aim.

The result will be that the pastor gets to be a psychotherapist, which again means that, unless he be a trained psychotherapist, he becomes a quack.

The most serious aspect of this situation is that soul care then no longer *is* soul care, as it loses its spiritual value. But this kind of "soul care" is unable to bring help where psychotherapy is in particular need of such help. This is demonstrated most clearly when the causal factors belong in the ethico-religious sphere.

A "soul care" which has surrendered its spiritual aim to psychotherapy is also unable to locate the tender spot under which the deepest ailment is found, where the Christian message is the only power able to heal.

The currents in our day that tend to efface the boundaries between soul care and psychotherapy should be carefully watched. The right course must be to let each seek its own channel, be conscious of its own history, learn from its own traditions, and reflect on its peculiarity.

Göte Bergsten of Sweden, in his book *Psychology and the Care of Souls,* p. 44, has the following noteworthy statement: "That which the Christian pastor of today is mostly in need of is not primarily a complementary course in psychotherapy, but, on the contrary, an ever-deepening insight into the various practical problems of soul care and a thorough familiarization with its wealth of experiences, in order that he may make a purposeful use of its possibilities."

Pastors of our day must, more thoroughly than ever before, take note of the essence and distinctive character of soul care, and make use of the unsuspected, limitless possibilities offered by soul care.

If a pastor neglects to do this he will receive scant help from a knowledge of psychology. Contrarily, he is in danger that his psychological erudition "will make him a singular, virtually homeless borderland dweller; one who may know more about psychoneuroses and their treatment than of the essential aspects of religious problematics; a pastor guilty of an uncritical transference of psychotherapeutic ideas to the religious field, one having more faith in 'psychological salvation' than in spiritual salvation" (Bergsten).

A one-sided, exaggerated interest in psychology on the part of pastors may result in a psychologizing both of their preaching and of their care of souls. Psychology is no gospel, but rather a means for serving the gospel. Here it therefore behooves pastors to be on the lookout.

Some try to make soul care and psychotherapy neutral concepts; they speak of religious and secular soul care—absurdities caused by a confusion of ideas. According to its essence soul care can be nothing else than *spiritual* concern, even though it includes both psychic and bodily life. When once in a while the expression *Christian* soul care is used, it is done for the purpose of stressing the specifically Christian aim of and the means employed in soul care. But, generally speaking, the adjective "Christian" is unnecessary in connection with the term soul care. By the same token the expressions "Christian" and "religious" are confusing when used with the term psychotherapy.

It is just as incorrect to speak of Christian psychotherapy as of Christian surgery, as both surgery and psychotherapy may be practiced by Christians and by non-Christians. On the other hand, we may speak of Christian surgeons and of Christian psychotherapists, i.e., surgeons and psychotherapists who confess the Christian faith.

The *other* view of the relationship between soul care and psychotherapy has as its main characteristic that it emphasizes the *difference* between the two. It contends that confusing the two will be detrimental to the mission of both, and also to those administered to. Consequently, the important thing is to make clear the essential differences.

A typical representative of this school of thought is the Danish physician H. I. Schou, M.D.

According to him, there is no essential connection between psychotherapy and soul care in the original meaning of the two terms. Psychotherapy is, above all, treatment, one to be carried on like all other treatments: on a logical, rational basis without regard for religious concepts. Treatment of psychic conditions, like treatment of corporeal ills, must be based on empiricism. Experiences under observation of human psychic conditions in sickness and in normal health must be the basis, combined with modern findings regarding the psychic structure: subconsciousness, psychic reflexes, repressions, etc.

By soul care Dr. Schou means: declaring the gospel to the individual. That is: to help the individual under differing situations, the young as well as the old, sick or healthy, man or woman, sinful or impeccable, guilty or acquitted—*under all circumstances;* and to offer him salvation in Christ on premises which he is able to understand or accept.

Dr. Schou contends that psychotherapy and soul care are totally different from each other. The former is a purely rational, humanistic, empirically conditioned manner of action, while the other is an offer of the power of God, a religious help from an irrational, transcendental world. "There is no bridge between the fields of action of the physician and the pastor, seen from the deepest point of view. The work of the one is of the world, that of the other of God."

He states, too, that psychotherapists cannot be prepossessed in favor of any moral tradition, any tradition, or any religious profession. It is quite otherwise with pastors. They are bound to the Word, to faith, to Christian morals—in brief, to the Book. Here the question is not the restoration of health, but man's eternal salvation or damnation.

He draws the line even more sharply in the matter of the pastor's or the doctor's relation to the ailing: It is the doctor's business to treat the psychic ailments, but it is *not* the pastor's. "When a man in travail of soul consults a doctor, then the latter is to deal with him as a physician, not as a Christian layman." And when a man with a psychic infirmity seeks a pastor, then the pastor is to minister to him as a Christian counselor of souls, not as psychotherapist. "In the matter of drawing clear lines for the future we must say: The physician's work with patients is separate and distinct, as is the pastor's work with sinners, but—in reciprocal co-operation."

We owe Dr. Schou much appreciation for the clear confirmation given by him of the relation between soul care and psychotherapy, a result arrived at after a thorough scientific education and training and after much experience and mature consideration of the questions involved. For many years he gave lectures on psychiatry to Danish pastors at the University of Copenhagen. For a generation he headed the great Filadelfia Institution at Dianalund and founded there the first and largest neurological sanatorium in Denmark. He is also a protagonist in the movement for cooperation between physicians and pastors in Scandinavia.

For this reason his words carry weight when he discusses these things. He was convinced that the time was favorable for cooperation by the two professions. He said: "We have begun to understand each other" (in Scandinavian idiom: We are within speaking distance).

It was for the very purpose of promoting a fruitful cooperation between the two that Dr. Schou deemed it so needful that "clear lines" be drawn. He was convinced that, both on account of the sufferer and for the sake of the practitioner's peace of mind, a demarcation line would be clearly followed to avoid confusion.

The conclusion drawn by Dr. Schou sounds clear and straightforward. Pastor and physician, each having his distinct field of labor, must keep their work separate and allow no confusion. True, Dr. Schou is much in favor of having pastors study psychology and acquire psychiatric information. The object in so doing, however, should not be to practice healing, but to seek equipment for two other ends: on the one hand, to refuse dealing with psychic ills and refer them to a physician; on the other hand, to achieve readier contact with the individual, understand his reactions, and thus help him to receive the gospel. I admit readily that I wholly agree with Dr. Schou in making a clear and definite demarcation between soul care and psychotherapy. His formulation in this respect will stand as a classic expression of the essential difference between the two.

But even so I am unable to rid myself of the feeling that something is wanting in his presentation; I feel that he has succeeded better in expressing that which separates the fields than in what they have in common. I rather think that Dr. Schou himself may be aware of this. The lacking synthesis appears in a suggestion of his for the creation of a third type of academician: "Psychotherapists having a thorough, comprehensive training in dealing with the soul. They need not necessarily be physicians, but, as for instance *masseurs,* be licensed practitioners and work only under a physician's assignment—university training being taken for granted."

But in its consequences this arrangement would also result in virtually making the pastor a psychotherapist, even as the pastor may, by "taking an additional course in psy-

chotherapy," turn into a psychotherapist. The problem of
finding the right relation between the two fields will in
no wise be solved by this device. The problems of soul care
are not solved by the pastor's becoming a psychotherapist.
In this way he may easily lose sight of his real aim and miss
it, and also, perhaps, be tempted not to employ the means
which rightly belong in soul care. It may also lead to the
obliteration of the clear lines which Dr. Schou so clearly
has pointed out. In some countries the results of such a
development are in evidence. As a rule soul care is the loser
in such instances, for greater emphasis is then laid on the
immanent rather than on the transcendental forces. The
fulcrum is then moved from God to man. However, a soul
care which no longer knows its own characteristics and has
lost sight of its aim, man's eternal salvation, is not soul care
in the truly Christian sense.

I deem it useful to have dwelt at some length on these
two widely differing ways of explaining the relation between
soul care and psychotherapy.

After evaluating these two ways we shall try to express
our own view of the matter. It is the result of many years of
intimate and fruitful cooperation between Norwegian physicians and pastors, as well as after many searching discussions on the relation between soul care and psychotherapy.

Chapter V

Common Ground

Responsibility Toward the Whole Man

The two distinct fields of soul care and of psychotherapy do not merely touch each other, nor do they shade over into one another in such a way as to form a common plane of contact. Such a demarcation between the fields would require a feat of equilibrium beyond the power of both pastor and physician to manage. History has showed that with this view of the situation the two professions have only come farther apart; in the end the only kind of contact between the two has become one of opposition and conflict.

No, soul care and psychotherapy have not only points of contact in common; they have *a common field of operation,* namely *man.* Both are designed to help man, our fellow man—not only a part of him, but the whole man, the personality itself. We cannot separate one part of man from the rest of his "organic" totality, for man is not a machine, but a living unity, one being. Viewing man as a totality has not always been marked in the Church's care of souls; on the contrary, this care has often been circumscribed, one-sided, directed only toward one part of man's personality.

26

I believe that one reason why clergymen often have had small success in cooperating with physicians and others who seek to help man on the plane of personality, is that they have not drawn the right inference from the Bible's view of man. Theology—the teaching about God—is not the only science which should use the Bible as its source and norm; also anthropology—the science of man—should do that. Anthropology and one's concept of man are decisive factors in the making of a pastor's personality and of his view of life, and also in his administering a correct and effective soul care.

The biblical view of man is determined by what Scripture relates about the first man, Adam, and about the last Adam, Christ. This is most clearly expressed in 1 Cor. 15:45: "Thus it is written, 'The first man Adam became a living being' *[psyche]*; the last Adam became a lifegiving spirit *[pneuma]*."

God's revelation in creation and in redemption gives us the whole and true picture of man.

The story of creation relates the following: "Then the Lord God formed man of dust from the ground, and breathed into his nostrils the breath of life; and man became a living being" (Gen. 2:7).—"So God created man in his own image, in the image of God he created him; male and female he created them" (Gen. 1:27).

Thus there are three things related to us in the Bible:

1. Man is an *act of creation* by God. "God formed man"— "He breathed . . . the breath of life." Man has his whole existence in God. Only through God does man become man. All of him—body, soul, and spirit—is in absolute dependence on God.

2. There is a difference between body and soul, but also a connection; there is an insoluble unity between them. The

soul is not a mere function of the body, but a separate and sovereign entity; and it functions as a superior and directing force in relation to the body—a circumstance, however, which does not belittle the body as an essential part of man. The body, with its wants and its instincts, is God's own creation. The sexual urge, for instance, is not something inferior of which we need feel ashamed, nor something in itself sinful which we are to despise. Rather, it is something sacred, instituted by God to be used according to his will, as a link in his plan for the furtherance of our destiny.

But man is not only body; nor is he only spirit. Spirit and body in organic unity constitute what the Bible calls *a living soul.*

That living soul has a *material side,* which connects it with the earth. The soul is unthinkable without association with the body.

But it has also a *spiritual side,* with attachment to the eternal and unperishable. In Hebrew this spiritual side is called *ruach,* the spirit of life. It corresponds to the Greek *pneuma* used by the apostle Paul. He follows the trichotomic division of the nature of man into *soma* (body), *psyche* (soul), and *pneuma* (spirit)—see especially 1 Thess. 5:23.

The Bible uses the term Spirit *(Ruach, pneuma)* both to denote God himself, who is spirit, and also *that* in man which points beyond the temporal, the corporeal, and the psychic.

The essential, the characteristic, with man is *spirit,* as it was as spirit-beings that God made us men.

3. Man was created in the image of God. What does that mean? It is not easy to comprehend, and to define it is difficult; but it is likely that it means an indication that there is something about man which *resembles* God, something which reminds of God. What does this mean? In the Bible

God is called by several names. For instance, in Ex. 3:14 God speaks of himself as "*I AM.*" God is a person—*ego sum?* That God created man in his own image must mean that man is an *ego sum,* a consciousness both of himself and God. "Also he has put eternity into man's mind" (Eccl. 3:11).* "They show that what the law requires is written on their hearts, while their conscience also bears witness and their conflicting thoughts accuse or perhaps excuse them" (Rom. 2:15).

The individual is so made that he possesses the possibility to acknowledge what is the will of God, to stand face to face with eternity, but also to enter into fellowship with the living God.

Being created in the image of God means that man is an accountable personality with freedom of choice between accepting and rejecting the salvation revealed by God. This responsibility is man's charter of nobility, expressing, as it does, the exalted, eternal worth of his personality. We are accountable to *God,* in all respects: body, soul, and spirit.

The great misfortune of man was that he did not fulfill his God-given destiny, but fell away from God. He *sinned,* by missing his aim, by breaking away from God. This disobedience brought about the most serious consequences in our relation to God, to ourselves, to our fellow men, and to the world. And in the wake of sin followed disease, suffering and death.

It is great to be a human being, but solemn as well. We can become God-like, but we can become like devils, too. Sin and demonic influences may master us; we may become worse than animals. It is possible for man to become allied either to Satan or to God.

---

*The latest Norwegian version has here: "Also *eternity* he has laid in their hearts." —Translator's note.

The view of man as a totality, while found in the Old Testament, is more clearly expressed in the New Testament, as it is revealed in its fulness in Jesus Christ, both in his teachings and in his life.

According to the Gospels Jesus did not make use of the trichotomic division of the nature of man, but the dichotomic: body and soul *(soma, psyche)*, and very often he employed the term soul in the sense of man in his entirety. Thus his view of the soul corresponds closely to that expressed in the story of creation: "And man became a living being."

It is in being thus a "soul" that man's great and eternal worth consists. "For what will it profit a man, if he gains the whole world and forfeits his life? Or what shall a man give in return for his life?" (Matt. 16:26). The most insignificant and least esteemed man is a soul of such great worth that the term vastly exceeds any known standard of values.

But the concern of Jesus for the welfare of the soul can not be separated from his thought of the body, even though with him *soma* and *psyche* belong together. He knew that sin was the deep and essential cause of the *soul's* distress, but also that the *body* suffered under the consequences of sin, as disease, suffering, and death had come in the wake of sin. Therefore he waged war not only against the devil, but also against everything *evil*, including sickness, pain, want, and death. In the salvation procured by him there is not only atonement for the punishment and guilt of sin, but also deliverance from the consequences of sin. This is proved by his power over disease and death and over evil spirits. Therefore, no one can understand and succor men better than Jesus Christ.

This makes it clear that the healing and other help which

he gave men did not belong outside of his mission of salvation, but were integral parts of it. All his actions were parts of God's plan for the salvation which men needed. His concern for men's bodily distress was inseparably bound to his concern for the salvation of their souls. His active love embraced the whole man, body and soul.

In this connection attention should be called to the fact that Jesus used the word "soul" in a sense somewhat different from that which today commonly is attached to the term *psyche,* which today is a definite concept in general use both in psychology and in medicine. Even though there is today no uniform agreement by way of a definition of the term, there is nevertheless a concensus to the effect that *psyche* does not exist only in an intimate reciprocal action with the body, but that it is a term for the conscious, the preconscious, and the subconscious life as it reacts and functions from birth to death, regardless of ethical and religious attitude. It is—in the words of a well-known psychologist—"an expression for the experiences and behavior of living beings."

But with such a conception of the *psyche* one cannot escape recognizing that in the psychic life there are forces beyond human power to control. There are forces outside of us that direct us and totally control us.

For this reason there are many psychologists who express the opinion that there is something irrational connected with the *psyche,* and also something pointing beyond psychic life itself. In other words, there is something more about the *psyche* than we can understand and explain, something beyond our power of scientific exploration. Here psychologists will usually maintain that this "something more" belongs in a sphere of existence other than that which pertains to psychological science, and that this is something extra-psychic belonging to metaphysics and theology.

Nevertheless, there are some psychologists who take cognizance of it, feeling forced to do so by experiences encountered in their efforts to help their fellow men. Among these is the Swiss physician and psychologist C. G. Jung. Dr. Eivind Berggrav, late Bishop of Oslo, discussed this matter in his book *Legeme og sjel i karakterliv og gudsliv* (approx. translated: Body and Soul in Relation to Character and Religious Life)—incidentally a most readable book. To quote in part:

"Jung does not hesitate to use the word God, although he is extremely wary over against all forms of metaphysics and theology. But he is forced to do so, he says. If one does not say God, there will, from the purely psychological point of view, be lacking something essential in one's characterization. He could, admittedly, express himself empirically and correctly, intellectually viewed, by the use of the term *autonomous content,* but only by the use of the designation God or something divine is he able to get explicitly brought out that which is the real *point* of the experienced content, i.e., this that here are forces in evidence which are *totally above us.* These forces and powers are just as important as e.g., hunger or fear of death. This power expresses itself within us through crossing our will, coercing our consciousness, and influencing our sentiments and our actions. This is not 'conscience'—it is *soul.* The individual *I* is sensible of itself as an object under an unknown and superior subject. Here, according to Jung, psychological facts compel us to go beyond the confines of present science. Without such a postulate the empirically occurring processes of the mind cannot be formulated.

"What is new here is: *that which is in the psyche is insufficient for giving it direction.* There are forces outside of us which scientifically must be designated by an x, but *they are there.* And their effect appears to us in such a characteristic moment as when strong psychic displacements reveal where the decisive points are found."

Returning to Jesus' use of the word soul, we note that in using it he wants to express, not merely something essential with man, but *the most essential.* The body may be killed, but not the soul (Matt. 10:28). Therefore, the salvation of the soul is more important than bodily health and psychic well-being. Jesus has given also many other clear expressions of this. The soul is the meeting place of man and God. It opens unto faith and life eternal. It acknowledges sin and guilt, and it receives forgiveness of sins.

If this is collated with Paul's view of man, we find that *soul* with Jesus means largely the same as *pneuma* (spirit) with Paul, and also that "spirit" is used in relation both to God and to man. Of God, the term the Spirit is used in the sense of the sustaining principle of life and of the imparter of life. "The written code kills, but the Spirit gives life" (2 Cor. 3:6). Through the Word of God the Spirit mediates God's life and salvation to men. The effects of Christianity are also attributed to the Spirit: "But the fruit of the Spirit is love, joy, peace, patience, kindness, goodness, faithfulness, gentleness, self-control" (Gal. 5:22-23).

Pneuma (Spirit) is also used about Jesus Christ. As "the last Adam" he has become *pneuma soopoiun,* i.e., "a life-giving spirit" (1 Cor. 15:45). Jesus is thus a spirit which makes alive. That corresponds to what he said of himself: "The words that I have spoken to you are *spirit* and *life*" (John 6:63).

But spirit is used, too, to designate that quality in man

which puts him in contact with God. Hence, *pneuma* is here something which points beyond psychic and bodily life. It involves the "boundary-exceeding tendency" (Berggrav). Spirit is that element in man which is absolute and eternal. As the organ of man's ethico-religious life it is "the meeting place of man and of God himself." The spirit can be obedient or disobedient to the Spirit of God; it can allow itself to be convinced by, open unto or close itself to the salvation of God. It is the spirit which opens unto faith and creates the Christian way of life.

The immanent powers of our *psyche* cannot lift us up to fellowship with God. Only the spirit can do that, and then only by contact with the forces of salvation revealed by God in Jesus Christ. Here we are face to face with the very crux of Christianity, as Christianity does not consist in our thoughts and ideas about God, but in the revelation of God's thoughts toward us and in the salvation given us in Jesus Christ. The heart of the matter is not our way to God, but God's way to us. His revelation is the only source and norm for the life of the *pneuma.*

In our presentation we shall abide by the New Testament's division into body, soul, and spirit. Luther defines it in this way: "*Pneuma* is the highest, deepest, noblest part of man, that which enables him to apprehend the invisible, the incomprehensible, the eternal. *Es ist kürzlich das Haus wo der Glaube und Gottes Wort innewohnt*" (It is, briefly stated, the house in which faith and the Word of God dwell). —And further: "*Psyche* is this *pneuma* seen from the side of nature, that is: everything which our reason acknowledges and can measure. Therefore in the *psyche*, reason is the great light; in the spirit, faith is the light."

In making use of this threefold division we shall use the word *psyche* in its usual psychological sense, in contradis-

tinction to spirit *(pneuma)*. On the other hand, "soul" will
often be used in the double sense. Sometimes it is used in the
same sense in which we have just now used "spirit," e.g., in
the phrase, "the salvation or the perdition of the soul." Then
reference is made to the eternal phase of the soul, that in the
soul which turns either to or from God.

I largely agree with Bishop Berggrav in his suggestion
that the word "soul" be reserved for the *psyche* in its functions as *pneuma*. Thus, the "soul" is that aspect of life in
which the reciprocal activity between God and man is found.
But in our continued presentation we may also, occasionally,
use the word "soul" in its double sense. It will then appear
from the context whether "soul" is used in its pneumatic
or in its psychic significance.

We have now seen how biblical anthropology regards man
as an insoluble unity of body, *psyche,* and spirit. As God has
so created us, his salvation encompasses the whole man.

Soul care does likewise. A soul care which does not recognize and meet its responsibility toward psychic suffering
and bodily need is failing its mission, and is no Christian
soul care. "As you did it not to one of the least of these, you
did it not to me" (Matt. 25:45).

Here is clear evidence that soul care and psychotherapy
should cooperate. In combating sickness and other suffering,
psychotherapy is doing God's work, as a means in his hand.
Thus, soul care and psychotherapy work together against a
common enemy. "Without a doubt there are many physicians
who, like me, have had the feeling, when combating an illness, of being face to face with an enemy, and that not a passive enemy, but an able antagonist skilled in the use of wily
cunning." (Tournier: *The Bible and Medicine,* Norw. ed.,
p. 111.)

In such instances the pastor will deem it a part of his

soul care to utilize the possibilities offered him by his service to assist the physician in his endeavor to bring the patient back to psychic soundness and bodily health. And this is legitimate soul care, as it belongs to the discharge of the responsibility and care which a pastor has toward the sick person. In this way both soul care and psychotherapy may be integrated as positive links in that organic unity which aims at helping the whole man, to achieve the re-erection, deliverance, restoration, and salvation of personality.

This common field of operation, the total personality, should be the foremost factor in the cooperation between the two professions. They need each other's help in maintaining this total view of man, particularly so in our day of strongly marked specialization. It is, of course, admitted, that specialization is a development which will continue, and which no power can stop. It should be noted that specialization in and by itself is not a danger—the biblical division into *soma, psyche,* and *pneuma* is here a case in point But the danger consists in detaching a unit from the God-given coherence of parts.

The sustained system of specialization in a modern hospital naturally brings it about that each worker is busily engaged in his own specific task, and he may then easily be tempted to forget the human individual. Scientific technique demands an ever increasing number of examinations and newer methods of treatment. This leaves little time to pay attention to the patient's person and to what may lie "back of the sickness." Knowledge of the patient gets to be more or less limited to that of his illness. The case-book is usually resorted to for information about the patient, who in this way may readily be only a "case" and not a person, a cog in a great machine. A well-known physician writes in one of his books: "Often the illness indeed is cured, but not the patient."

The one-sided symptomatic treatment may become a temptation both to pastor and physician. Some people hide their neurosis back of religiosity. They may be punctilious in their religious observances and strict toward others. As a rule, they seek pastoral counsel readily, but their religiosity is only a screen for what may often be a serious illness.

Likewise there may be symptoms of illness which cover a serious spiritual hurt.

The discovery of the real cause of an ailment will be made easier through a natural and intimate cooperation between pastor and physician, and in that way real help may be administered.

In such cooperation, however, many others also make telling contributions, notably among the many others employed in a hospital. Some work in the wards, others in the operating room, laboratory, X-ray division, office, kitchen, etc. Everything done is a part of the whole. All concerned are to have a common aim in their work: to give the patients the help needed. Collective action is here the watchword for all, for doctors, pastors, nurses, social workers, psychologists, attendants. Each individual is a unit in the larger organism, a member of a working team. If the individual is to perform his special task, there must be interplay of actors, no discord. Being dependent of one another, each one must willingly aid his neighbor. If each worker is animated by a spirit of helpfulness and love, then this spirit will characterize the whole hospital. The most important asset of a hospital is its spirit, its atmosphere.

The objective must be to assist the whole man. Body, soul, and spirit are bound together by means of both visible and invisible ties, and between them there is an interaction which indeed can be observed and studied, but which lives beyond the possibility of scientific comprehension. The reason for this is that there are depths in the human personality which no one can sound. Only God knows what dwells in man.

But that interaction within human personality which men can investigate is given us as a problem for solution, in the interest of human welfare. In this investigation the pastor should not be concerned only about spiritual conditions, because there are many spiritual troubles, such as insecurity, doubt, depression, travail of soul, which may have other causes than unbelief and other sins. The causes may have to be looked for on some other plane—in the person's surroundings, in his constitution, in either psychic or bodily weakness, suffering, and disease. In such cases help is needed not only in the spiritual, but also in the psychic and bodily sphere as well. Here is required in a special way an intimate, effective cooperation between physician and pastor.

The pastor must be able to refer the afflicted person to the sources of power accessible for restoration of psychic health and for cure of bodily weakness and disease. But even if bodily healing cannot be achieved, and psychic difficulties cannot be wholly overcome, the pastor must earnestly seek to help the patient to react in a positive way and to gain power in his weakness and suffering.

But the psychotherapist, too, must be aware that in his treatment he should aim at the total personality, something which he cannot do without taking into account the ethico-religious factors in the case. The question here does not concern itself with the psychotherapist's personal attitude in religion, for it may range from atheism all the way to personal faith in Christ. But here is a legitimate demand for respect for the patient's faith and view of life, for spiritual values.

If the psychotherapist ignores the spiritual aspect he will be unable to help many persons whose special difficulties belong just in this sphere; for experience has demonstrated that the ethico-religious factors play a prominent part in psychic ailments. Psychosomatic symptoms are not always sure indications that the ailment has organic causes; they may as readily be caused by something which has happened on the ethico-religious plane. The cause may be a repressed feeling of guilt, a moral defeat, a spiritual breakdown, or a sin unconfessed; it may, too, have connection with an unsatisfied religious need. (See also Chapter VIII.)

Dr. Jung wrote as follows after thirty years of practice with neurotic patients:

"Among all my patients beyond 35 years of age there has not been a single one whose indefeasible problem has not been one of religious attitudes; indeed, all of them have become ill because they had lost that which a living religion always contributes to its confessors. Neither has any of them regained his health without having regained a religious attitude, a circumstance which, as a matter of course, has nothing to do with confession of or attachment to a definite church."

Personal Contact

A common concern for pastor and for psychotherapist is that they succeed in establishing personal contact with the person whom they desire to help. Personal contact is the bridge or conduit which is to transmit and effectuate the help which the patient needs. Without such a contact the work of both pastor and psychotherapist is in vain. And contact is necessary not only in the transferring situations in soul care and in psychotherapy, but generally in all kinds of situations of a personal nature.

In this matter we are dealing with something of essential and crucial importance in the work of soul care and psychotherapy. There is a certain amount of anxiety and suspense connected with dealing with a new patient, with a new acquaintance, for that matter. Will contact be possible? Will psychotherapist or pastor succeed in establishing contact?

How is contact established? There is something irrational connected with the process. Really, it has more to do with *emotio* (emotion) than with *ratio* (reason).

A common experience for pastors and psychotherapists should be a personal attachment to their work and to their fellow men. They are to meet others on the personal plane and discuss with them the most intimate human experiences, a situation which inevitably must challenge and engage our attention and interest.

Contact!—That is something which concerns our personality! Establishing personal contact does not primarily depend on whether he who is to establish it is either a pastor or a physician, but whether he is a personality able to create contact. If that requisite is present, then he who is seeking help may with equal profit confide in the one as well as the other, whether it be the pastor or the physician. (Further discussion of this is found in Chapter IX.)

Interviews

The conversations carried on by the pastor and by the psychotherapist with the health seeker have also much in common.

Spiritual life is not an isolated domain in human personality, as it produces both bodily and psychic effects and, in fact, permeates our whole being. As a result of the reciprocal action of body, soul, and spirit, as well as the interplay among them, there is not a single sphere of life to be regarden as alien to soul care. This being so, both pastors and psychotherapists are often confronted with the same experiences, situations, sufferings, difficulties, and problems. There may be problems dating back to early childhood, or having occurred in the upbringing, at home or in school, or in the place of work; or they may have relation to economic and social hardships, to sickness and adversity, to sexual involvements, or to marriage conflicts.

Naturally the pastor and the psychotherapist will see the same things from different points of view. The latter will primarily inquire into how the things brought into the conversation will react on the psychic and bodily well-being, while the former will in the first place be interested in the effects on conscience and faith, on spiritual life in general.

There is an organic connection between pastoral and psychotherapeutic interviews, much as body, soul, and spirit belong together in the same person. The aim in both cases should be to reach the total personality in the talks carried on with patients by both professions.

Pastors and psychotherapists will also have much the same experiences in meeting defeats, difficulties, and struggles, but they will, too, have many of the same kind of joys and encouragements in their contact relations and in their conversations with patients.

Chapter VI

Differences

If a good and profitable cooperation between soul care and psychotherapy is to be established, it is not enough to clarify the matter of common ground between them; recognition of their differences is also of importance.

We shall therefore proceed to discuss three things which separate them. In the matter of arriving at a clear view of the division of labor involved there are differences in the *objectives sought* and in the choice of *means of labor,* and there are also differences in the matter of *vocation.*

Objectives Sought

The difference between soul care and psychotherapy may perhaps be most plainly and simply expressed by the use of two words: salvation and health.

The objective of soul care is, first and foremost, the salvation of men, while for psychotherapy it is psychic soundness and bodily health.

Soul care, too, is interested in the health and well-being of the body and in soundness of mind. We have earlier emphasized the responsibility which soul care has over against bodily and psychic need. But the eternal salvation of man is for soul care far more important and decisive than achieving health.

Soul care has a different and larger perspective than psychotherapy. While the latter is anthropocentrically directed the former is theocentrically directed, and it regards man's relationship with God the most essential. It accounts sin and grace, salvation and perdition, heaven and hell as absolute, non-realizable concepts.

According to what has earlier been stated, soul care has a much wider scope than psychotherapy, for soul care deals with both a healthy and an unhealthy soul life, with the whole of man. Therefore it has larger and wider dimensions than psychotherapy. This is most noticeable when psychotherapy has reached its limit in helping a patient. The case may be a hopeless one, as seen from both the medical and psychiatric point of view. But soul care will continue to deal with such a person in faith and hope, as both of these are confident that what is impossible with men is possible with God. The wider dimension of soul care is especially seen face to face with death, as faith in Christ gives eternal life, power and victory in death, comfort in sorrow, and help in affliction.

While soul care thus has a wider perspective, it also concentrates more markedly on the one thing needful. It has a stronger interest in the *quality* of life than in the *quantity* of it, i.e., its chief concern is not in *how long* a man is to live, but in *how* he is living. Soul care takes into account that there is a purpose in suffering, and also realizes that learning to react rightly to sickness and suffering is far more important than getting well. God has a purpose and a plan for every sufferer. The important thing is to discover this, and then to act according to God's will.

For psychotherapy, psychic soundness is the greatest, but for soul care truth is greater than soundness.* And soul care seeks to help people to find truth—the truth about themselves and about God, in all situations of life. And truth revealed in Jesus Christ is objective. It will meet man both as an authoritative, obligatory message and also as a liberating force. "You will know the truth, and the truth will make you free" (John 8:32).

As truth cannot be separated from love, so the biblical saying: speaking the truth in love, must always be the rule in soul care.

While it is true that soul care has a message to bring, it must never force this on people. Its purpose is to assist the individual to make his decision as far as possible on the basis of personal responsibility.

But in very many situations people do need assistance in making their decisions, as for instance in situations of conflict in which decisions of very serious and far-reaching consequences must be made. We need mention in passing only such situations as: prevention of conception, *abortus provocatus,* sterilization, insemination, leucothomy, separation, divorce, etc. There may be clear medical indications of the necessity for having something of the kind done. Nevertheless the final decision may not be easily made by the person directly concerned, or by his relatives. Many cannot view the case from the strictly medical point of view, as it is for them a matter of conscience, a question involving their relation to God, their salvation.

In such cases they may feel that the doctor's advice is insufficient, and so they turn to their pastor in order to become assured in conscience that their decision may be

---

*The Norwegian has here an interesting play on words: truth is *sannhet,* and soundness is *sunnhet,* Translator's note.

according to the will of God. They want to be assured that they act in keeping with God's Word. Very often they will ask the pastor directly what the Word of God says or what their church teaches concerning the problem facing them.

Where the medical indications are clear and unmistakable, giving advice is not so difficult. Often the clear biological truth is seen to be in agreement with ethico-religious truth.

It is far more difficult to advise when the medical indications are not so clear, when physicians' findings vary, especially when they are diametrically opposed to each other. The pastor must take care not to mix into medical controversies; he is neither a physician nor a psychotherapist. But it is his clear duty to answer such questions of conscience which a bewildered, suffering fellow man puts to him. The purport of his answer must clearly belong on the ethico-religious plane and must be in clear agreement with the Word of God. But his answer belongs only in the category of counsel, not of command. It is for the individual himself to make the decision; and both for him and for the pastor the decisive norm must invariably be a conscience bound by God's command in the Word.

Different Means of Working

The tools, or means of labor, differ according to the results desired. Psychotherapy makes use of the means which medical science from time to time provides (see pp. 6-7), whereas soul care has the means given the Church: The Word of God, the sacraments, confession, prayer, and Christian fellowship (see p. 13).

There is a fundamental difference between these means.

The psychotherapeutic means belong on the horizontal plane and take account of immanent powers. Forces transcendent: miracles and absolute, eternal values, lie outside the field of psychotherapy. By its means it is not searching for truth in the metaphysical sense of the word, but for health in a biologic-psychologic sense. That does not mean that psychotherapy is not interested in ethico-religious values and factors, and in their significance for psychic health. A denial of this would be a case of scientific impertinence, and it would indicate a materialistic-dogmatic view of life.

For also a psychotherapist will recognize the value and significance of the means of soul care, but only to the extent to which ethico-religious influences will be an aid to health. In a primary sense he is, as a psychotherapist, not interested in the salvation and ethico-religious transformation which soul care seeks to bring about. As soon as he proceeds to use the gospel and other means which belong to soul care in his psychotherapy, he is to that extent no longer operating as a psychotherapist, but as a Christian, in reality as an administrator of soul care. In this connection it should be remembered that soul care, in its widest sense, is the duty of every Christian. There is really no contrast between the responsibility for witnessing laid upon all Christians and the special calling into pastoral counseling given within the Church to certain individuals.

The means of soul care have not only a different mission, but also a different kind of effect than the means of psychotherapy, as they operate vertically, having their origin, source, and power in God, and seeking man in his actual situation. "Soul care is not accomplishing its mission until a man, in all respects, faces God and heeds his Word" (Fjellbu).

Fundamental among the means of soul care is the Word

of God; it furnishes the underlying basis in all relations. But of great importance, and extensively used in everyday soul care, are also prayer, conversation, and private confession.

Many sick folk have difficulties in their *prayer* life and are in need of counseling, help, and encouragement. Most of them want very much to regain their health, and many, indeed more than we usually think, pray God to heal them. Therefore, a burning question with many, one often encountered in soul care, is healing through prayer. When faced by this question the pastor is in great need of tact and clear thinking, of wisdom, above all of fidelity to the Word of God. Perhaps the foremost need here is showing that prayer is not a means of healing; if it were, it would belong rather to psychotherapy than to soul care. Prayer is primarily given us as a means of getting into fellowship with God, as it gives us access to the fountain of salvation and to eternal forces. It is not a means for gaining our own desires, for advancing our egotistic plane, but it does open up to us unheard-of, boundless possibilities for furthering God's will with us. And, healing from sickness has a part in the will of God. This means that we must be willing to use the means and ways which the Bible shows us; i.e., we must leave it with God to hear our prayer *when* he wills, and *how* he wills, by those means and in the way which he deems best.

It is of importance to emphasize here that there is no contradiction between healing through prayer and the use of natural means of healing, but an interaction and a co-operation.

Conversation used in the care of souls has—as stated earlier —many points of likeness with psychotherapeutic conversation, the difference lying, essentially, in purpose, aim, and methods. It will, at all times, aim at the salvation of the whole man, even if this aim may not always be directly expressed in words. The pastor's intuition and intercession, his whole attitude, must have its course, inspiration, and renewal in the spiritual means whence he has his own life. This heart-to-heart talk with the patient must have its centrality in the Word of God; everything must be seen from its point of view. Guidance and counsel must correspond to the revealed Word. As long as soul care is real care of souls it is bound by the Word and will seek to help men conform to it. The purpose of conversation in soul care is to make clear God's answer to the individual in the concrete and factual situations which he faces.

Confession. Not all conversations in soul care terminate with the use of the confessional. It is not pertinent—as some maintain—to place such conversations and private confession in juxtaposition, as conversations always have a wider reach than confession and in that way avoid even the semblance of psychic coercion toward confessing sins. Confession must always be a spontaneous matter, a wholly voluntary moment, never to be induced by outward, human influence.

At this point there is a sharp cleavage between the means and methods of soul care and those of psychotherapy. Narco-analysis, or an active depth analytic method to disclose something of value for bringing about psychic health, is recognized as a legitimate psychotherapeutic means, but not so in soul care. A confession must come wholly voluntarily and naturally, as a result of a spiritual and psychic maturing process in the conscience.

In the last instance only the Spirit of God can create in the heart a consciousness and confession of sin. The act of confessing in the private confessional comes, therefore, as a fruit of the Spirit's action in the heart, for which reason confession has its natural place among the means of soul care.

Let it be noted that confession is not a device invented by man, but is founded on and enjoined by the Word of God. As such it has always belonged in the Church, although it has at times been much neglected, to the great hurt and loss of the many who were thus deprived of its power and blessing. For private confession can work healing both physically and psychically, although healing is not all there is to confession, but only one of the effects it may bring about. Its intent lies on the spiritual plane: in absolution and in appropriation of the forgiveness of sins.

Confession contains, to wit, two parts: acknowledging of sins, and absolution. This presupposes a confessor, and, on his part, an obligation of secrecy or silence, the reason for mention of which is obvious. A pastor who breaks this solemn pledge of silence can be defrocked. It may often be necessary and salutary that attention be called to this strong safeguard placed about the confessional, in order to create a feeling of security and confidence on the part of the penitent.

Although in the confessional the penitent confesses to another human being, the confession is essentially a confessing of his sins to God; only it is done in the presence of another.

The most important part of confession is the absolution, i.e., the declaration of forgiveness of sins. While it is true that confessing one's sins is a necessary prerequisite for receiving forgiveness, one is not given remittance of guilt *because* of his confession, but solely because he accepts and believes the pardoning word. The form of absolution may vary a bit. It may take the form of a direct quotation from the Bible, or it may, more commonly, be done by the laying on of hands and the use of the ritual pronouncement:

"By the authority of God I declare unto you the gracious forgiveness of your sins in the name of the Father and of the Son and of the Holy Ghost."

Experience has given evidence that both ritual and authority play a large part in this connection. The following story is told by a well-known German pastor, Johann Christopher Blumhardt, the leader of a mighty awakening in Württemberg. The first man who sought spiritual help from him, a man of ill repute in the village, asked him whether he thought there might be forgiveness for such a man as he. Wanting to test the man's sincerity the pastor told him that he had better confess to him, at which the man hesitated and left. But he soon returned, and during his third call he yielded and made confession. However, after absolution he remained depressed; no words of assurance seemed to help him. "He said," Pastor Blumhardt tells, "that he felt that unless I absolved him on the strength of the authority vested in my office he would not get any peace." Blumhardt answered that he doubtless would feel more comforted on his next call. But when the man called the next morning he was still depressed, and he again voiced his desire for a formal absolution according to the words of the ritual, which the pastor then gave him, with the laying on of hands. "Then," writes Pastor Blumhardt, "when he arose from kneeling, his face had a wholly different expression, beaming with joy and thankfulness."—The news of this man's confession and transformation spread rapidly, with the result that the pastor was virtually overrun by requests for confession with subsequent absolution.

It would appear that private confession has been rediscovered, and that it will receive more of a revival long overdue. Also within the Lutheran Church "this matter has increasingly become a unanimous *pium desiderium*" (Gustav Jensen).

That the means of soul care are transcendentally and vertically orientated does not mean, however, that they have no horizontal effects. It is a fact that soul care does work healing both in sick bodies and sick minds. But it should again be stressed that health of body and soul is not an aim, but always an *effect* of soul care, and that healing takes place by virtue of the means characteristic of the care of souls. A pastor has no right to make use of medical or psychotherapeutic methods unless he, in addition to his pastoral training, has the training of a physician; but, if he has, he must use these methods as a physician or a psychotherapist, not as a pastor. The drawing of clear lines is *always* the best policy

Different Vocations

In our presentation we have maintained that soul care and psychotherapy are two distinct vocations, each with specific purposes differing from those of the other. The question may be raised whether this is the right view. May not soul care and psychotherapy be administered by the same person? It can not be denied that this is possible, both theoretically and practically, for one having the professional training and the personal qualifications called for in both spheres. There are physicians who ably perform soul care, and there are pastors who have psychotherapeutic gifts.

But in practical life it has been demonstrated that each of these vocations demands a person's full time and attention. Granted that they have much in common, it is nevertheless true that each has a main calling so distinct that a man must, in the final instance, decide for the one or the other. There are physicians who have chosen to become pastors and preachers, but then they ceased their medical practice and devoted their full time to the ministerial office. We also know pastors who later on trained themselves for the medical profession; they were not able to keep up two vocations, but left the ministry and gave their full time to the practice of medicine, or to some specialized service in this field.

It is therefore right, both from the practical and the theoretic point of view, to uncover the distinctive element of each of these vocations: clergyman and physician, pastor and psychotherapist.

In this connection mention should be made of the old-time family doctor, who for generations administered both psychotherapy and soul care, in the best sense of the words, without being a specialist and professionally trained for either. He is greatly missed, as people long for the presence of an understanding, sympathetic consultant. Here is a marvelous field of service for the pastor of today, if he will take sufficient time to establish real contact with people. Even though we may not get the family doctor back, we may, perhaps, get pastors who become real family ministers in the homes.

Chapter VII

Cooperation

Though psychotherapy and soul care are not identical, the relation between them is, as we have seen, one of organic and inseparable connection, the practical result of which is the need of an intimate and effective cooperation. Experience has proved that this is possible. There need be no friction between them, since they are so essentially different in purpose, means, objectives, and bases that a competitive comparison should be unthinkable. "Asking which of the two has the pre-eminence is just as senseless as asking whether penicillin or communion is preferable in dealing with a patient." He may be in need of both.

Soul care and psychotherapy are neither competitors of nor substitutes for each other. No question of rank or prestige is here involved. Their mission is to work together for the amelioration of human ills. In some instances they may pass over into each other by easy gradations, e.g., in such a way that soul care may be the psychotherapeutic help needed by the patient or vice versa. But cooperation is the order of the day.

This cooperation will result in a common joy for psychotherapist and pastor when they succeed in helping a fellow man to achieve psychic well-being and health. There should be no question about which one brought about the best result, because often it is not easy to determine which factors are the most decisive in any given case, nor to state which was the most momentous agent in the healing process. The all-important thing is that something *real* takes place. There are many participants in teamwork, and each one has an important part in the great cooperative effort aiming at the final healing of the individual. It is for each worker to be aware of his limitations and restrictions, and of his specific task, above all: to be at the same time humble and cheerful, and to show respect for his fellow worker.

Such cooperative effort not only creates a common joy and encouragement, but it also develops a common sense of need, face to face with sickness and suffering, with destructive and evil forces. Contact is established with people in dire need, engaged in solving difficult problems. This will often lead to a searching self-examination and to a challenge both for pastor and for psychotherapist. At times they may be tempted to despondency because the suffering encountered is so great, the situation so difficult, the problem seemingly so unsolvable. One feels so personally committed in this work because one is so closely involved both with the other person's need and with the outcome of the undertaking.

For this reason physician and pastor, and patient as well, are in need of each other's assistance in an open, trustful work-fellowship, which often develops into a pleasant comradeship. In a cooperation on the personal plane one cannot remain detached, but must rather be willing to subject one's own reactions to self-examination. But after talking things over with a fellow man it may be profitable to spend a little time alone in quiet reflection. In this way one may discover faults and mistakes in one's own conduct, a circumstance which may be of benefit to the patient, to one's fellow workers, and to oneself.

Often the sharing of difficulties and problems with a co-worker, a doctor, or a pastor, will be of value.

The manner in which cooperation between members of the medical staff and of the clergy will work out depends on many things; among these, working conditions play a big part. There are noticeable differences in the circumstances under which clergymen work, whether it be at a hospital, a psychiatric institute, or as a parish pastor. A full-time hospital chaplain is integrated as a regular part of the hospital organism and he functions under its administration and routine. This is an advantage in that patients get accustomed to seeing and meeting the chaplain in the same way as they meet the physicians and the nurses. Being thus afforded an opportunity to come into close contact with the patients, the chaplain is enabled to meet them, as a fellow man, in a natural fellowship on an ordinary conversational basis. This associational contact between patients and pastor has often opened the way for pastoral contact. The fact that the pastor thus is regularly seen at the hospital, and not at occasional visits only, as for instance when a patient is noticeably failing, may counteract the false notion that the arrival of a pastor is a sure indication that someone is very seriously ill. Soul care is not merely for patients about to die, but just as much for those headed for recovery.

I want, in passing, to call attention to the findings reported late in 1955, of a committee appointed by Norway's Department of Church and Education to study the work of chaplains at about 80 percent of Norway's hospitals. The committee was made up of a chief-of-staff, a hospital superintendent, and a chaplain. From this report made by the

chairman of the committee, a well-known physician, I quote
the following findings:

"It appears from the material gathered by the committee
that there is a general recognition of a great demand for
pastoral services—for soul care—at our hospitals. There are
only rare exceptions to this expression of opinion collected
from head doctors and head nurses. Thus, there would seem
to be a wide recognition at our hospitals that a great latent
religious need exists.

"I have stated earlier in this report that there is, generally speaking, unanimity in regard to the question that
pastors ought to represent the Church of Norway in our
hospitals, and that worship services, devotions, and administration of the sacraments ought to be conducted to a warrantable extent. The Church ought to be present in our
hospitals, at the disposal of those desiring its services. The
Church may have such a position at the hospitals without
incurring special conflicts and difficulties even where the
hospital administration may be alienated from the Church,
since every sensible management will recognize the religious
needs of patients, even though the administrators themselves
may not share these. The general good-will evidenced by the
material indicates, I believe, a special relation to the official
functions of the Church. Our findings also indicate a realization of the pastor's significance for the individual patient."

Cooperative action between hospital chaplains and physicians will express itself in many ways. The circumstance that
it manifests itself as a natural part of the whole exerts a
positive influence on the general personnel of the hospital,
and certainly on the patients. In some places this becomes
marked when physician and pastor occasionally make a joint
call on patients, but even where this is not the custom the

consciousness of the existence of cooperative action by the two will open the way for and make easier establishing pastoral contact with the patients. And as a member of the working team the chaplain may participate in staff meetings, in the review of cases, and in the discussions of common problems.

The supreme principle in every hospital must be that every effort put forth is to promote the health of the patients; and in this central objective soul care has its share. Even though it operates along its own line and has its own special aim, it nevertheless seeks to help the sick to attain health and psychic soundness. For God is not only the God of salvation, but also of health and well-being. As stated earlier, perfection of health is included in the perfect salvation. It is the final result of the death and resurrection of Christ. Promoting human health and well-being belongs to realizing the will of God with us. The pastor must, therefore, in his cooperation with the doctor be willing to submit to a mutual supervision and control to the extent that these are designed to and are able to promote psychic health.

In the pastor's talks with the patient and in confession circumstances may be revealed which in the pastor's opinion will have a bearing on the patient's psychic and bodily health; the patient's interests will then be served by the pastor's acquainting the physician with these circumstances. It follows as a matter-of-course that, whenever necessary, the pastor should ask the patient's permission so to do.

A live question for the pastor, and one of interest also to the psychotherapist, is when and where soul care ought to begin. Is it for the pastor or the psychotherapist to decide time and circumstance? Experience has taught me that the problem is solved most advantageously through frank and open teamwork. And effective cooperation will clear away conflicts and other difficulties which otherwise might arise.

The functioning of soul care does not presuppose only a normally sound psychic life. It cannot be relieved of responsibility also for a sick soul life, in such a manner that it leaves it altogether to the psychotherapist to decide when the treatment of the psychic ailment has progressed far enough to allow soul care to begin; for, as already stated, soul care is concerned not only with sound psychic life, but with the whole person, also when ill. It recognizes a latent ethico-religious need in *all* men, and no one knows how much of such a need may exist within a sick soul life. Further, experience shows that the Word of God possesses a power of its own to penetrate into even the weakest and sickest *psyche,* indeed into the mind of imbecile and incurably insane persons. The same has been observed in some cases of unconsciousness. The subconscious mind may be open to religious impressions; persons so sick that they no longer recognize even their nearest relatives may suddenly become awake when they hear a familiar Bible passage or a stanza of a beloved hymn.

Nor must it be forgotten that the terms sound or sick soul life are relative concepts not always easily diagnosed or defined.

The Word of God is absolute, working in spite of the extent of our comprehension, and more deeply than we are able to fathom and search out. "For the word of God is living and active, sharper than any two-edged sword, piercing to division of soul and spirit, of joints and marrow, and discerning the thoughts and intentions of the heart" (Heb. 4:12).

I shall never forget an experience I had while studying psychiatry for a time at the Psychiatric Clinic in Oslo, under Professor Ragnar Vogt, M.D.

A woman had asked me to call on her husband who was

a patient at the clinic. Because of his illness it seemed practically impossible to establish pastoral contact with him; he
was so apathetic as to be almost inapproachable. One day
his wife asked whether I would give him communion. I cannot now remember what I answered, but I was much astonished at her request, having serious doubts whether I could
do it or not. I had no spiritual scruples, for I knew that the
man before his illness was a professing Christian; but I was
held back thinking that it could in no way profit the man in
his enfeebled condition.

In my bewilderment I consulted the physician in attend-
ance, a man whose religious attitude I did not know, but with
whom I had had pleasant cooperative associations. At my
question, he seemed much surprised that I as a pastor was
doubtful about what to do under the circumstances, motivat-
ing his answer by saying: "Remember that *every* patient has
a full right to have his religious needs satisfied."

His answer helped me, and it also solved a problem for me.
I shall always feel indebted to the physician (later a professor of medicine) for his counsel. It is the pastor's foremost
duty and absolute right to try to meet the patient's religious
needs regardless of the nature, form, and stage of his illness.
In this respect the pastor is answerable, not to man, but to
God.

But this duty does not include a pastor's right to call on a
patient both in and out of season. There will be situations in
which he ought to stay away, knowing that the patient's
present greatest need is medical attention. As a sick
psyche is in need of healing it is the mission of soul care to
help the patient to recognize and to accept his illness. In his
cooperation with the doctor the pastor will regard it as his
part to be of assistance to the doctor in just that which he is
trying to do. This is especially important when the patient

confuses sin and symptom, something particularly noticeable in cases of depression, neurasthenia, fear neurosis, and
melancholia. Psychic weariness is then confounded with
spiritual indifference and lukewarmness, fears caused by illness with self-reproach and self-condemnation. A person
suffering from melancholia is likely to be harassed by false,
sickly guilt feelings, fears of impending doom, and fears of
having committed the unpardonable sin.

In such situations even a pastor must advise abstention
from the regular use of the means of soul care. For instance,
the reading of the Bible will then only result in distortion
of its meaning. Such a patient once said to me: "I am to be
cast into the lake that burns with fire and brimstone." Upon
my asking who had told him so, he said, "I have read it in the
Bible, and the Bible is God's Word."

Keeping the Bible from patients at such times does not
mean that the words of the Bible are to be taken from them.
For they are particularly in need of the message from God,
the very word which they then must not read. It is then to
be given them by *others*. Just here is a great opportunity for
pastor, doctor, and nurse.

That the pastor in many situations must wait until the
psychotherapist deems the time opportune does not constitute a slight toward soul care, nor a denial of its necessity.
It is only a consequence of the needed natural cooperation,
with a division of the tasks, in the interest of the common
field of labor, the total man. The pastor must train himself to
wait for the opportune time for beginning soul care, until
the need for pastoral care has been actualized, until conditions for a spiritual ripening process are ready.

This may be compared to a farmer who is about to sow
his seed. He does not scatter the seed haphazardly. He
must first clear, plow, and also otherwise prepare the ground.

Casting the grain on stony or barren ground is a waste both of seed and of effort. Much the same preparation must take place in our soul life: Much clearing and tilling need be done. Here I am reminded of the words of the Bible: "Prepare the way of the Lord, make his paths straight. Every valley shall be filled, and every mountain and hill shall be brought low, and the crooked shall be made straight, and the rough ways shall be made smooth" (Luke 3:4-5).

This is the work of psychotherapy. Its aim is to heal the sick psychic life, correct derailments, strengthen the weak, and combat negative, destructive forces in the *psyche*.

This procedure is in keeping with the practice of Jesus in his care of souls. Usually he first cured the ailment, relieved temporal want, cast out evil spirits. Then he gave spiritual help and salvation.

When psychotherapy contributes toward making a highway for spiritual values, thus making it possible for these to operate, it is directly engaged in the service of the Most High. The well-known German psychiatrist Professor J. H. Schultz, M.D. (the founder of the "Schultz training"), writes that psychotherapy is meant to be a means in the service of soul care, paving a way for it through professional skill. He maintains that man's highest good and all values that deal with faith and transcendent life do not belong to psychotherapy proper, but assort under soul care. "*Zu diesen höchsten Werten durch Beseitigung krankhafter Störungen in medizinisch-psychologischer Facharbeit den Weg zu eröffnen, das allein ist die Aufgabe der Psychotherapie*" (To open the way for these highest values through adjustment of sickly aberrations by medical-psychologic professional skill is alone the task of psychotherapy).

But when the pastor, as compared to the psychotherapist, plays, as it were, a waiting, passive game in these situations, it does not mean that he is inactive and passive in his own sphere. He is always to show his active concern for the patient through following the work of the psychotherapist with keen interest and with professional evaluation of it, and also through loving, sympathetic intercession for the patient.

The pastor must be concerned constantly lest he drift into rigid methods and schemes in his work. Here he must take care to learn from the Master's example. He acted as he was needed in each individual instance. Thus it was not always that he first healed the sick person and then spoke his saving word; sometimes he reversed the order. A case in point was when a man sick of the palsy was brought to him. There was nothing to prevent him from saying first to the man, "Arise, and walk," but he did not do it. On the contrary, his first words were: "My son, your sins are forgiven." For the man was ready to receive the spiritual help which Jesus from the beginning wanted to give him. The Lord knew that the man was receptive to the declaration of the forgiveness of sins.

In a similar way both pastor and psychotherapist must learn to recognize and utilize the opportune moment. In this school are needed intuition and spiritual alertness, and also sensitiveness and obedience of spirit over against the psychic and spiritual reactions of the patient.

We move here in a realm which makes men feel small and humble, but also grateful for being deemed worthy to be instruments in the hand of God for service to our fellow men.

Physician, psychotherapist, and pastor are united for working together as a unit, much as *soma, psyche,* and *pneuma* work together in a unit named man.

At a congress of psychiatrists and pastors an American physician made use of a drastic, but striking illustration. On his way to the meeting place something went wrong with his automobile, which then had to be taken to a repair shop. The car mechanic readily found what was wrong and repaired the damage. But when the traveler asked the mechanic for directions about the route through Europe he was advised to go to a travel bureau. There he was told the right road. This illustration he made use of in the following way: When one's bodily functions fail, a physician is consulted. When one's psychic functions go awry, one is sent to a psychiatrist. But when in quest of the purpose and meaning of life, one had better turn to a soul counselor, who on the basis of the Bible would give the answer of the Word of God about the way, the truth, and the life.

Some of that which has been stated above about cooperation between pastor and psychotherapist concerns not only hospital chaplains, but every pastor giving counsel to souls. The difference is not here one of principle, but belongs to practical conditions. It is, of course, true that a hospital chaplain has a much greater opportunity for cooperation with psychotherapists, as his associations with them are of a systematic, organic, and intimate nature. While the chaplain is in position to devote his whole time and energy to such cooperative effort, the parish pastor has many tasks demanding his attention in an extensive, well-organized parish ministry. Every minister is called both to preach and to give direct counsel to souls. But the forms and opportunities for preaching and for soul care usually differ in the case of the hospital chaplain and the parish pastor.

In every parish there is a great need for counseling conversations and for confession. Many of those filling doctors' waiting rooms ought also to fill the offices of parish pastors. Besides those who consult doctors there are many others, too, in need of an intimate talk with a soul counselor.

I have not the least doubt that, if the need for soul care which exists in our parishes would be met, our pastors would have more than enough to do every-day counseling with people in need and with hearing confessions.

What are the reasons that conditions are not such? The situation is, quite simply, that those in need of soul care are indeed plentiful, and also that there are those capable of giving it. One reason why the needy do not come to receive help is the lack of contact. We cannot discuss this at length, but I shall point out a few things which may bring about a greater contact.

It is of primary importance that practical possibilities for easy access are provided. The office or study of the pastor should be designed with this end in view. The first requisite is that the interview may take place without outside disturbance or interruption, and in such a way that the natural shyness of a depressed soul may not unduly prevent him from seeking the interview. If the pastor is summoned by telephone or by knockings on the door during the interview the one seeking help may easily get the impression that he is making undue demands on the pastor's time. And a pastor's counseling room should have a separate entrance.

In cities the pastors have, as a general rule, their offices in the church or in the parish house. The official office hours could afford opportunity for soul care consultations; but the time is usually too short, and other calls on the pastor are too many, to allow enough time for soul care then. It is therefore better that such interviews be arranged for some other time. Announcements should also be made at church services and in the columns of the parish paper (perhaps also in newspapers) that people are welcome to seek counseling appointments.

But of still greater importance is the *regular* establishment of the practice of soul care in the parish. If it is generally known that people have received help through private consultation with the pastor, the existence of such a need will then evidence itself through requests directly made to the pastor, through telephone appointments, or through letters.

Finally, how may a pastor manage to meet this need? Here we are face to face with one of the basic questions encountered by a pastor, not only as seen from the practical angle, whether there is sufficient time or not. The question is rather to what extent a pastor is to give priority to counseling interviews in his ministry. Viewed from the point already taken in this presentation that soul care and preaching are contiguous and organically united, the answer should not be far to seek. Let it be remembered what a prominent role soul care played in the work of Jesus; he was always ready, both day and night, to help seeking souls.

Returning directly to the matter of cooperation between pastor and doctor, let it be said that there are not a few physicians and psychotherapists who desire such a cooperation. But also *pastors* must want it. Something definite must be done by both sides to establish such a contact. During late years this contact relationship in our country (Norway) has been enlarged through numerous conferences between physicians and pastors, with courses in and lectures on soul care and psychotherapy, and there have in many localities been a greater cooperation between the two professions. But even though a good start has been made, much remains to be done. Each side must seek to increase this cooperation for the benefit of patients and also for mutual help and inspiration.

Pastors must try to clear away obstacles which keep people from coming to them for help. For instance, we must arrange our office hours on as practical a schedule as do the doctors. One of the latter made the following suggestion: "There should be set aside definite hours, at least on four days of the week, so that everyone may know that the pastor's office is then reserved for pastoral consultations, and not for any other business." There can be no doubt that there is a need for some such arrangement. But to make this possible, pastors must give soul care a priority which it so far has not had—and this will require many more pastors.

A question pressing for an answer in this connection is to what extent pastors in general are equipped for soul care service.

It should be admitted that the regular course in theology lays as good a foundation and provides as adequate a preparation for our candidates for the ministry to become soul care counselors as the regular course in medicine furnishes basis and equipment for medical practitioners to become psychotherapists.

In addition, our theological students hear lectures on psychiatry at one of our leading institutions for mental patients, by a university professor; they are also given a course in neuropathology. In this way our future pastors are given an introduction to recent findings in psychiatry and psychotherapy. This is of great value to them in evaluating cases of psychic disturbances which they may meet later. Thus the student will learn to distinguish between sound and unsound psychic life. And such a knowledge will naturally lead to contact and cooperation with physicians and psychotherapists.

Students of theology are given also a six weeks' course in clinical soul care at one of the leading hospitals in Oslo, directed by the hospital chaplain. Since 1951 the hospital has given a three months' course in soul care and psychotherapy, mainly for pastors. The course embraces both practical and theoretical instruction. Students are afforded the opportunity to give soul care to patients, supervised by doctors and chaplains; to participate in staff meetings, in case reviews; and to hear discussions between psychotherapists and soul counselors; also to become acquainted with modern methods of psychiatric treatment, and to learn the most important results of contemporaneous psychotherapeutic research.

The theoretical part of the instruction consists in having the students hear lectures in psychiatry at the aforementioned mental institute or at the Psychiatric Clinic. A hospital chaplain lectures on soul care, and reviews cases and conducts general discussions. Reading of specified literature is assigned. A number of pastors take this course. And several pastors have sought further education along the same lines abroad.

To the training and qualifying of pastors for soul care service an acquisition of necessary acquaintance with psychology is needed, a science which naturally gives needed aid to a soul counselor. This is especially true of depth psychology. In at least one instance depth psychology's significance for soul care has been likened to the significance of the discovery of X-rays for medical diagnosis, and to the possibility of deep X-ray radiation for medical therapy.

But of greater importance to the soul counselor than a theoretical knowledge of conscious and unconscious psychic life is the possession of a psychological insight and a perceptiveness enabling him to get the right contact with his fellow men for rendering help at the right time.

At this point I want to emphasize knowledge of human nature and understanding and wisdom of the *Bible* are important. Many a time I have been deeply impressed by the

manner in which a man or a woman without scientific training (i.e., neither a theologian, psychiatrist, nor professional
psychologist), by the aid of common sense and familiarity
with the Bible, has been able to render decisive help and to
gain access where a person with educational training has
failed.

This is not so strange, for the Bible does impart knowledge
of human nature, perceptiveness, and wisdom. Every one
who deals with sick and suffering persons ought to study
the Bible thoroughly—the Book of Job in particular. Note
carefully the following quotations from Job 28:20-28:

" 'Whence then comes wisdom? And where is the place of
understanding? It is hid from the eyes of all living, and con-
cealed from the birds of the air. Abaddon and Death say,
"We have heard a rumor of it with our ears." God understands the way to it, and he knows its place. For he looks to
the ends of the earth, and he sees everything under the heav-
ens. When he gave to the wind its weight, and meted out
the waters by measure; when he made a decree for the rain,
and a way for the lightning of the thunder; then he saw it
and declared it; he established it, and searched it out. And
he said to man, "Behold, the fear of the Lord, that is wisdom; and to depart from evil is understanding." ' "

Chapter VIII

Therapy of Pastoral Care

We have discussed above that the essential *aim* of soul care belongs on the spiritual plane, but also that its *effects* inevitably are found on the psychic and somatic. Even though its aim is salvation, its effect is health.

As soul counselors we do not desire to set off these effects in a special way, but merely to state a fact concerning them. Soul care does not need to advertise itself. A publicity-seeking, obtrusively boasting soul care does damage to its purpose and is a hindrance in the way of producing good results.

Neither does it need to defend itself against attacks, for its calling is not that of an advocate for its cause, but that of a true, authentic witness. Soul care must be conducted quietly, cautiously, and tactfully in order not to impede the forces it sets in motion.

The effects of soul care do not come as a result of human performance and display of power. "God is at work in you." Rather, the effects grow out of the inner, hidden pneumatic life. "The fruit of the Spirit is love, joy, peace, etc."

When we now proceed to mention a few of these effects,

it is done only for the purpose of bringing about a truer conception of the nature of soul care. It is then natural that we first make mention of soul care as a *spiritual force.* That which characterizes soul care is its spirit, its tone and atmosphere, that which causes it to give rest, security, and peace. Through it the weary finds rest, the fearful security, the vacillating a sure foundation, one that will remain firm under the vicissitudes of life.

This is corroborated from medical quarters.

Professor Ragnar Vogt states in his book on medical psychology and psychiatry: "The fears and annoyances of life disappear when a person is able to find a meaning in life. The Danish poet B. S. Ingemann sings about the peace of God as the never-setting sun of the soul."

Another well-known physician, H. I. Schou, a man who has spent a lifetime working among nervous and mentally afflicted persons, writes: "From my practice I could mention a considerable number of instances showing that neurotics have been cured when placed in the right *milieu,* and when they, through a sympathetic soul care, have had their religious longings satisfied. There is healing in religious experience, and rest in Christian faith."

Soul care also gives poise and a personally appropriated view of life. In a lecture on "Nervous Breakdowns in Our Time" Dr. Per Anchersen of Oslo stated: "With all due respect for medical progress and for modern social welfare work, the value of which can not be overestimated, I am, nevertheless, of the opinion that a personally appropriated, thoroughly studied view of life, in which reason and faith fuse, and when the petty things of everyday life are seen in a meaningful connection, may be a greater stabilizing factor than we usually are aware of."

I am, in the main, of the impression that psychiatric scientists evaluate soul care as a positive, healing factor. Dr. Schou, mentioned above, has in his books listed many expressions to that effect by world-famous psychiatrists. I shall here quote only a couple of these. Professor Oppenheim says: "A strong, firm faith is a protection against most of the agitations which the vicissitudes of life bring about within those who lack this foundation."—And Professor Kraft-Ebbing says: "In the main it must be held that true religion, pure ethics, ennobles the spirit of man and directs it toward a higher goal, gives comfort in misfortune, and lessens the danger of mental disturbance."

Correction of Misconceptions

Many persons entertain religious misconceptions which often aggravate their suffering, and even their disease itself. It is the mission of soul care, through Biblical guidance, to help in removing some of these stones in the path of the sufferers.

The Sound Doctrine. In this connection I wish to call attention to an expression used by Paul in some of his epistles; he speaks of "sound doctrine." The words for *sound* in the original text are *hygiaino—hygies—hygea,* whence our medical term hygiene. Paul speaks about being sound in faith, in love, and in patience. The sound doctrine is unadulterated doctrine, which does not deviate from truth. We have earlier noted that *sannhet* (truth) and *sunnhet* (health) belong together; for, if we adhere to the truth revealed in the Word of God, truth will bring about health. Just think if we had lived according to God's commandments, or in dead earnest had tried to keep the one commandment of love: to bear with one another, to forgive one another, to love one another—what perspectives would have opened! What consequences would have followed! How many conflicts, tragedies, disasters, pests, distresses, and wars would have been avoided!

The sound doctrine presupposes the existence of also an *unsound* doctrine, one not in keeping with the Word of God. This kind of doctrine will work harm both to body and soul. It is the mission of soul care both to prevent such washouts on the track of life and to help those derailed back on the right road.

For instance, there are people who hold that all forms of nervousness have their cause in religious conditions; they maintain that psychic ailments come because the person concerned is not "right with God." I mention a few instances: "I have asked God to take away my fear, but in vain." Another, who suffered from sleeplessness, said: "Both my husband and I have long prayed God to restore sleep to me; but it doesn't look as though he hears us. I have been hospitalized, too, but that hasn't helped either."

And so temptations thicken, causing spiritual darkness. "Why doesn't God hear me? Is it because I have not enough faith? Or, perhaps, because I may not really be a child of God? If I were a child of God, really and truly saved, then God would have heard my prayer and helped me. I understand now that I am not right with God. But I am so disappointed, and I am tempted to become bitter."

What can soul care do in such cases? It is not enough merely to tell the patient plainly that these things are symptoms of his sickness, and that they will disappear when the psychiatric treatment has taken effect. True, it is important to instruct the patient in the nature of illness; but it is also important to give him insight into the spiritual connections and implications. He should be told that to be a Christian is not the same as to be spared bodily and nervous suffering. God has not promised that we are never to be sick or in distress because we are saved and believe in him. It is possible to be a child of God and in the right relationship to him, and at the same time feel weariness, fear, guilt, sickness, and insomnia. Sleeplessness and fear are in themselves no proof that God refuses to answer our prayers— he answers in a way different from the one desired and expected by us.

The soul counselor is charged with the right and the duty to declare, concretely and directly, the grace, love and faithfulness of God to the individual in his actual condition. The sick one has the right to believe his sonship with God in spite of darkness and temptations. And such a faith and encouragement may contribute toward dispelling some of the delusions which stand as hindering factors in the way toward healing.

Sickness, Punishment, Atonement. Another idea that may arise during sickness and distress is the temptation to think of one's sickness as a *punishment* for sin.—"What wrong have *I* done that I am visited with this sickness? Why should it come to *me?* Is it because I am so much worse than others? Maybe it *is* meant as a punishment for my sins? Or, perhaps there are sins in my life so much worse than I know of? Anyway, I don't understand what God means by punishing me in this way."

Others look upon their suffering as an *atonement* for their sins. They are conscious of a great need for atonement, and they think that this must be met through hardships and tribulations on their part. The solution to this problem they seek through stoic resignation, through submission to their inevitable fate, no matter how hard it may be. When such notions become imbedded in the mind, they will easily produce negative reaction in the *psyche* and rather aggravate the illness.

How does soul care deal with such conditions?

It is not possible in our comparatively brief presentation to discuss exhaustively such serious and vital problems; but we shall briefly indicate the answer of Scripture. The most lucid answer has been given by Jesus Christ himself. Once some people came to Jesus to tell about some Galileans who had been shockingly massacred, the inference being that those concerned must have been greater sinners than others. Jesus said, "Do you think that these Galileans were worse sinners than all the other Galileans, because they suffered thus? I tell you, No." Thus the answer of Jesus was a categorical *No*, which told them that they were wrong and had entirely misunderstood the situation. Jesus expressed himself on this issue even more clearly on the occasion when he had healed a man born blind (John 9:1-38). Wishing to learn the reason back of this man's hard fate, the disciples asked, "Rabbi, who sinned, this man or his parents, that he was born blind?" In reality they thought they knew the answer beforehand: the cause of the hardship was somebody's sin. But Jesus rejected the idea of an immediate relationship between the man's sin and his hard fate, saying: "It was not that this man sinned, or his parents, but that the works of God might be made manifest in him." By saying so Jesus did not mean that those people were without sin; but he wanted to make clear that the answer to the riddle of human suffering is not found in the idea of retribution. Even if there is some truth in the assertion that suffering is punishment for sin, there is, nevertheless, a total misunderstanding of the entire issue in looking for *the* answer to the riddle along this line of reasoning. The complete answer we can dig out neither from our own conscience, nor from our thoughts and our experiences.

The solution is laid bare in Jesus Christ. The meaning of suffering belongs on a different plane than that of retribution: "That the works of God might be made manifest."

The punishment for sin is not something which we can remove either by suffering or atonement on our part, but it is something which Jesus has laid on himself. "He was wounded for our transgressions, he was bruised for our iniquities; upon him was the chastisement that made us whole" (Isa. 53:5). The message of the Bible is that Christ has done this in our place; he has atoned for our sins and blotted out our guilt. And because of this he has also dominion over the consequences of sin, over sickness and death.

The meaning of suffering is, therefore, to lead the individual to Jesus Christ. Then the works of God are made manifest in us, both unto healing and unto salvation. Jesus offers every man a way *out* of suffering, or *through* suffering to the goal, which is fellowship with God.

Misunderstood Bible Passages. There are many passages in the Bible which are hard to understand, and very often these are wrongly interpreted, in which case they may create big problems and psychic pressure in sensitive minds.

An unmarried woman was hospitalized because of what might be called a light case of depression which, according to indications, could be cured in a comparatively short time. But something kept troubling her, causing the depression to continue. She said she could not tell the physicians the nature of her trouble, but in a talk with the chaplain she finally opened up. In her early youth she had had a spiritual awakening which led to assurance of God's grace; she had experienced a freedom and joy hitherto new to her. This she confided to her mother, who was a professing Christian, but also very serious and highly susceptible. While she was thankful for what her daughter had told her, she was also somewhat fearful lest her experience had not been deep enough; so she said to her daughter: "Do not forget the solemn words of Jesus, 'For many are called, but few are chosen'" (Matt. 22:14).

To begin with she recalled her mother's words only rarely and gave the experience little thought. But every time she became spiritually troubled with uncertainty and doubt, then the experience came to mind, particularly the solemn words which her mother had quoted. And she began to wonder whether indeed she was *chosen*. Such periods of spiritual darkness made her very depressed, but she told no one of her distress. While relations with her mother had earlier been one of open confidence, this inner contact was now broken, and she became conscious of an aggressive attitude toward her mother, although relations between them otherwise remained good. Often she felt an urge to talk over things with her mother, but she lacked courage to do so. Some time before she went into her *depressio mentis* (for which she was hospitalized), her mother died. Very likely her mother's death, followed by grief and an added feeling of guilt, were contributory causes of the depression; at any rate these circumstances made her spiritual condition seem still more hopeless. And she felt now wholly convinced that she was not among the elect, but was forever rejected by God.

The telling in detail of the procedure and content of the soul care given her would be too involved, but suffice it to mention the three foremost items of the conversations. The soul counselor first stressed the positive element in her situation: that *now* she was having the opportunity of speaking openly about matters which she should have cleared up shortly after the episode with her mother. He also under-scored that her depression was not a punishment for sin, but wholly a natural reaction to the experiences she had been through.

Her second difficulty was the aggressive feeling against and the—more or less—negative attitude toward her mother; these gave her a feeling of guilt for which it was now too late to ask forgiveness. It distressed her greatly that she no longer had the opportunity to talk things through with her mother.—The declaration of the forgiveness of sins and private confession solved the guilt problem for her. She was able anew to believe that through Christ her fellowship with God was re-established, and that thus all her sin and guilt were taken away.

The third matter dealt with the Bible passage which she had misunderstood totally. The pastor had to explain to her its true meaning. There were also some other things dis-cussed, but the three items mentioned above were essentially those that had a decisive significance for her spiritual salva-tion and psychic health.

The passage mentioned above, Matthew 22:14, is not the only difficult statement regarding election. Sayings equally hard to interpret are found in Romans 8:29-30; 9:11 ff.; and in Hebrews 6:4-6 and 10:29; difficult is also the passage about "the blasphemy against the Spirit" (Matt. 12:31).—Note that "*Sin* against the Holy Ghost" is not a biblical expression.

1. A difficult passage must not be separated from its con-text, but must be considered in connection with the situation under which it was spoken.

2. The particular passage or section must be interpreted in association with what the Bible otherwise teaches. The Bible is God's revelation of our salvation; and the way of salva-tion is plain and clear. "It shall be called the holy way and

fools shall not err therein" (Isa. 35:8). There are no conflicting lines in the Bible regarding the way of salvation. This
fact should cause us to take alarm when someone, basing
it on some detached Bible passages, formulates a doctrine
in conflict with the Bible's dominant teachings.

3. The Bible's statements about election are given as a
word of comfort to the children of God, but as a solemn
warning to the indifferent. Fear of being lost is not an indication of spiritual death, but rather one of life, with those
who desire to be God's children. About this Luther has said:
"The tempted should find comfort and strength in this that
this fear is, in fact, a sign of his being foreordained to salvation, as one may be sure that they who are ordained to
judgment would not be able to have such thoughts and
fears."

Paving the Way to Healing

There are some sick folk with such an irrational view of
medical science and natural means of healing that they are
prevented from being benefited by them. They motivate this
view on religious grounds, maintaining that God both can
and always will heal them without medical treatment. If we
are to help such people we must meet them on the level
where the real hindrance is lodged.

A patient was in need of being operated on for a serious
ailment, but she refused to consent to an operation when the
surgeon told her of her need. She said that an operation was
unnecessary, for God could heal her through prayer. She
maintained this opinion also in a talk with the hospital chaplain. She had better leave the hospital, she said, and get in
touch with someone who could pray for her. The pastor

told her that she need not leave the hospital to get someone to pray for her, as he had often prayed for patients.
Her answer was that she meant intercessory prayer for sick
folk as prescribed in the Bible, particularly in James 5:14,
where mention is made of anointing with oil in the name
of the Lord. When the pastor then said that he practiced in
keeping with the Bible, she expressed great surprise that a
state church clergyman did that. But this brought about contact between patient and soul counselor, and established
confidence on her part. And it opened the way into an open,
effective soul care conversation. They discussed in a straightforward way what the Bible says about healing through
prayer, and she was led into a truer and saner view, which
in turn helped her to regard the natural means of healing
as means in the service of God. She was prayed for and
anointed with oil in the name of the Lord, through it gaining
spiritual succor: rest and confidence.

When the surgeon called again and once more suggested
an operation, she willingly acceded. The operation was suc-
cessful, and she returned to her home well and happy. She
looked upon her restoration as the work of God, but also on
the surgeon and the operation as the means he had used.

Some patients develop a neurotic repression which pre-
vents their getting into contact with physician and psychotherapist, while they, on the other hand, readily agree to
see the chaplain. In such cases the first contact is established
by him, leading on to such soul care as the circumstances
will permit with subsequent contact with the doctor.

For illustrative purposes I mention a patient in his middle
thirties, an intelligent man, very well educated; but upon
admission to the hospital he was, practically speaking, in a
psychotic condition, marked by religious delusions and
ecstatic experiences. He refused absolutely to be examined

by physicians, insisting that his first need was to be absolved by a soul counselor from the ban under which he felt himself placed. He held that he was absolutely forbidden by God to unbosom himself to anyone but a pastor.

The physicians having advised, as the first step, an interview with the hospital chaplain, this was arranged, resulting in the establishment of a promising contact. Several interviews followed, and the patient adjusted well to his hospital surroundings, but continued to refuse to see the doctors.

During the many and frequent talks with the chaplain he had the opportunity of unburdening himself of his religious experiences and difficulties, and also of his sexual conflicts. He showed himself increasingly receptive to soul care counseling. And as he gradually gained tranquility of mind, the chaplain was able to show him that he had confused *pneuma* and *psyche* and had mixed up cause and effect; he had been unable to differentiate between sickly and normal reactions in his religious life. It was fairly easy then to help him acquire insight into the nature of illness. And at length he admitted that what he had interpreted as divine guidance and spiritual experiences really were impulses of repression and unsound ecstatic states of mind. He was also open to conviction when he, soberly and clearly, was shown that his religious ideas were delusions caused by erroneous interpretations of the Bible (particularly of sections of Heb. 6 and 10).

As his strongly emotionalistic experiences receded in his consciousness, he began to react normally both in his religious and psychic life. "In the hospital he was a satisfactory patient, and toward the end of his stay there his contact with the doctors, too, was good. On dismissal he showed no psychopathic indications, but was naturally a bit uncertain about his future."

This patient has now been working normally for several

years; he feels entirely well and enjoys good contacts with his fellow men.

The necessity of administering soul care manifests itself also in many sex neuroses or in neuroses where sexual life at least plays a large role.

In a physician's course of treatment a shut-in situation may develop which makes further treatment impracticable. That may mean a stoppage in the healing process. The cause may be a decision to be taken before further progress can be made. The decision may relate to one or another of many problems, such as sterilization, *abortus provocatus,* prevention, sexual adjustment, etc.

Based on medical indications the doctor may have given definite advice in a given case, but the patient may demur, and raise objections, usually on ethical and religious grounds, as for instance: "Is it right to be sterilized?—Is it not a sin to remove the fetus?" In many of these cases the patient is not helped by the doctor's declaration that under the circumstances it is not a sin; but the situation is quite a different one for the patient if the soul counselor can say: "This you may do with a clear conscience, both over against God and man; it is not a sin."

In circumstances of this kind some patients have greater confidence in the pastor than in the doctor. The reason may be the difference in the calling and professional competence of the two men, each being a specialist in his own field. The case in reverse would be: That the pastor under given circumstances would feel convinced that nothing was the matter with the patient and would say to him, "You are not sick." The patient would hardly believe him. But if the doctor would say the same to him, the situation would be a very different one for him, since he would know that the doctor could speak with professional authority.

But if the pastor would neglect giving the needed soul care to patients in doubt regarding what decision to make under the circumstances described above, it would likely have unfortunate consequences. In my experience as a counselor of souls I have dealt with people suffering from a harassing feeling of guilt because they had acted on medical advice contrary to their inmost, holiest convictions. Or, they were at the time not spiritually and physically mature enough for making a decision which to them seemed coerced. An interview with a soul counselor at the right time is likely to clear away situations which otherwise might lodge in their soul life and produce spiritual and psychic complexes and repressions.

It is an essential part of effective cooperation between physician and pastor that they help each other in bringing about good results for the patient.

Some physicians may, perhaps, hesitate a bit about sending a patient to the pastor under the above-mentioned circumstances, as they may fear that the pastor's advice might lead to the patient's not getting the medical attention which they know is needed. This fear is groundless. For countless instances of soul care administered will show that where medical indications support the doctor's advice there the cooperative action of the pastor will be beneficial both to physician and patient.

I want in this connection to mention the large group of people having marital conflicts. Many of these find it easier to open up to a pastor, a circumstance which may have several causes. Some prefer to consult the pastor who officiated at their wedding, perhaps because the personality of the pastor appealed to them and created confidence, or because the conflict itself has ethico-religious implications;

then again many will find it more natural and easy to talk things over with a pastor than with a physician.

We have above mentioned some instances of *traumata* lodged in the soul life. Whether the religious experiences are contributory *causes* to the psychic distress or *symptoms* of it, is not always easy to determine. To investigate this is primarily not the task of the pastor, but of the physician. But it is a part of the pastor's work to help in releasing tenseness and psychic distress. He can penetrate into the religious *trauma* and also show the way to release and salvation. In such situations I have often thought of the one log which during the floating of timber gets lodged, thus hindering the entire raft from moving on. It is then the business of the raftsman to find this log and to dislodge it. This, too, is the business of the soul counselor in the area of soul life.

Ethico-Religious Suffering

Most clearly are seen the psychotherapeutic effects of soul care when the essential reason back of the psychic distress lies on the ethico-religious plane.

The suffering may have been induced by an unsatisfied religious, or by an unsolved ethical conflict because of unconfessed sins, by an unsatisfied religious demand.

A man in his fifties was admitted as a patient in a hospital section for internal medicine, suffering with pains in his stomach and also in other organs; these had hindered him greatly in his work for several years. After an exhaustive examination the doctors had to state that they could find no organic basis for these pains. A psychiatric examination was not suggested, as no indications pointed in that direction; and the man was about to be dismissed from the hospital. But before that was done he had a somewhat lengthy conversation with the chaplain, with whom he had established a good social contact. They discussed among other things what might be the cause of his distress, especially as the doctors had found no organic disease nor anything essentially abnormal in his *psyche*. The chaplain then, shunting the talk over to spiritual matters, suggested that the reason might be found in that sphere. The man's first reaction was a bit negative, but the chaplain noted that his thoughts had evidently been arrested, for which reason the chaplain tried to be as passive as possible, awaiting further developments. And after a while the patient said that there was something that he wanted to tell.

Ten years earlier there had been a religious awakening in the community in which he then lived; many came under conviction of sin and were converted to faith in Christ. He, too, was among the awakened; the Spirit of God convinced him of the true way to salvation and a new life. But he lacked the courage to act on his conviction. "But now I realize that I did the wrong thing then, and since I have had a deep sense of guilt, which has constantly tormented me."

In the talk which followed he unburdened himself of his gnawing feeling of suppressed regret, and it was established that his bodily pains had begun at the time of his spiritual refusal and had continued since. He was led to realize that he had consciously repressed his spiritual need and had left it unsatisfied.

Wholly spontaneously and voluntarily he now asked for spiritual guidance, which the chaplain, as a matter-of-course, gladly gave him, resulting in a full surrender to God on the man's part.

A very noticeable change took place in the patient's physical condition, something which his doctors also noted. After discussing the case with the chaplain the doctors concluded that the primary reason for the man's pains must have been the condition which had come to light under the chaplain's talks with the patient.

Such experiences in the cooperative work between physician and clergyman do not occur merely in hospitals, but also elsewhere, e.g., out in country communities.

A woman out in the country, about forty years old, had gone into a psychotic stage. As it proved impossible to get her to a hospital, the local doctor ordered watchers over her, since she was very restive. By nature she was quiet and reserved, keeping her troubles to herself. She had many children. Her husband had become dissipated and had ceased to provide for his family. Wanting to shield him from neighborhood criticism, she had taken on extra jobs in order to keep want from the home. By working night and day she had managed to keep things going without outside assistance. She was a wholly exceptional type of person, self-sacrificing, intelligent, and psychically well equipped. But at last the burden proved too heavy, she had a nervous collapse, which turned into a psychosis, marked by depression and melancholia. Early in her sad condition the doctor got in touch with the rector of the parish, and together they conferred about what should be done. When her restiveness subsided somewhat the rector began to call on her, and had many interviews with her.

These disclosed that she had during many years felt a deep religious need; she was, in other words, spiritually awakened, but had never arrived at assurance of peace with God. In her depressed state all these things pressed on for a solution. And the soul care given her not only gave her a chance for unloading her troubled mind, but also brought her rest and peace through the forgiveness of sins in Christ Jesus.

In a surprisingly short time her psychosis disappeared. She became a happy, liberated, confessing Christian, harmonious and poised in spirit. She went back to her household duties, an even more devoted mother than before. She was also able to adjust herself to her straitened circumstances because of her husband's failure as a provider, now accepting without embarrassment the outside aid which she badly needed. It was especially touching that she voluntarily began to take part in the work of the parish, offering her services to the Sunday school.

The many years of normal life since her breakdown show that her religious experience was genuine and dynamic.

I also wish to cite an incident told by a Danish physician, Dr. Ruth Poort, in a lecture which she gave in 1957 on the topic "Forgiveness of Sins, Responsibility, and Guilt":

"I once had a patient, a woman of about thirty, who had become apathetic and paralytic after the death of her child in an accident of which the mother indirectly was the cause. Shock treatment had not helped her. Neither had the many attempts to explain away the tragic accident which well-meaning neighbors, relatives, and friends had tried to comfort her with: 'You were not to blame' or 'You know it was an accident,' etc. But no such attempts availed; she remained apathetic, and desperately unhappy.

"At last I said to her, 'Don't you want to see a pastor about the matter? For you *were* to blame, you know; you were the cause of your child's death. But there is such a thing as forgiveness, God's forgiveness. Do you believe in God? Do you have connections with the Church?'

"She said she didn't know—she had, of course, been baptized and confirmed, but she had not been in the habit of attending church. But, on second thought, she would like to see a pastor.

"And she did. A week later she left for home, well. Her guilt had been taken seriously."

A German pastor has told the following incident from his work among mental sufferers:

"A young farmer lay in bed in catatonic rigidity. His stupor seemed to be increasing. His limbs did not move at all, not even his eyelids. Nourishment could be given him only through a gastric tube. Standing by his bedside one had the feeling of looking at a dead person, his reactions were *nil*. I stooped over him and said slowly: 'Fear not, for I have redeemed you; I have called you by name, you are mine' (Isa. 43:1). The attending nurse only laughed. After a few weeks the stupor began leaving him; he moved, and began to speak. To me he said, 'That Bible passage came to me as a lifeline thrown to one about to drown. On account of the pessimistic remarks which I had heard while I lay helpless, I thought that I should be buried alive. But then came the word from God that he would not forsake me.'"

Conscientious Scruples. "A domestic scene—fireworks of passion—often consumes more 'nerve energy' in a few moments than does steady work engaged in for a long time. The greatest wear is perhaps occasioned by conflicts not 'made up.' The making of a definite decision, grief, the death of one dearly beloved, are, very likely, less exhausting than some weeks fraught with suspense and dread. Sorrow produces sickness less often than supposed, at least not to the extent which conflicts, fear, and indecision do" (*Mental Hygiene*, 1937, p. 20).

Conflicts not settled may be cleared up through open discussion with subsequent settlement, and through counseling. It usually falls to the lot of a pastor to take part in such discussions in the varying everyday situations; and a hospital chaplain likewise, not only with patients in the psychiatric division, but also in the medicinal and surgical sections.

A patient who had earlier been operated on for a stomach ailment complained that his "old" symptoms were reoccurring. After an examination by the surgeon in question, who found nothing indicating the necessity for renewed surgery, he was transferred to the division for internal medicine, but also there no organic trouble could be found. During these examinations he was called on by the chaplain, with whom a good contact was established, and to whom he disclosed that during the entire time that the annoying symptoms had been felt he had suffered under compunctions of conscience because of an unconfessed sexual experience which he knew was a breach of ethical conduct. A feeling of guilt of which he could not rid himself was constantly troubling him; no operation, no medical treatment could remove it.

But after he confessed and made up with the parties concerned, and received God's forgiveness for his sin, the painful symptoms disappeared, and he became a new man. A few days later he was dismissed from the hospital as a cured case.

Unconfessed Sins. We have earlier *mentioned* private confession; here we want to *emphasize* its importance for psychic health, although the psychotherapeutic effects of confession are so commonly recognized that there may be need only of mentioning it. It is a well-known matter how the Roman Catholic confessional and also confession as practiced by other churches have helped millions of people.

On that account it is not necessary to give instances from everyday experience here. Besides, confession's obligation of secrecy and its intimate nature make such telling difficult. (As a matter of course nothing can *ever* be told without express permission of the penitent.) But one instance *can* be given, as it is told in the Bible. It is the classic story of the fall and restitution of King David. After his fall he lived through a period of bodily weakness and of psychic distress, of which the Bible tells the following, using his own words: "When I declared not my sin, my body wasted away through my groaning all day long. For day and night thy hand was heavy upon me; my strength was dried up as by the heat of summer" (Ps. 32:3-4).

We are also told the cause of his organic and spiritual distress. David had fallen victim to a temptation to have sexual intercourse with a married woman, Bathsheba, who became pregnant as a result. And when David learned of her condition he brought about the death of her husband.

Thus David had many sins on his conscience: adultery, unfaithfulness, murder, dishonesty. For a long time he covered up his guilt; that is expressed in his "When I declared not my sin." The Bible narrative makes it plain that he repressed his feeling of guilt (known technically as *regression*), that there was no open and conscious admission in him of the evil that he had done.

The prophet Nathan was sent him to give him the soul care he was so badly in need of. The Bible has the following graphic account of what he told the king:

" 'There were two men in a certain city, the one rich and the other poor. The rich man had very many flocks and herds; but the poor man had nothing but one little ewe lamb, which he had bought. And he brought it up, and it grew up with him and with his children; it used to eat of his morsel, and drink from his cup, and lie in his bosom, and it was like a daughter to him. Now there came a traveler to the rich man, and he was unwilling to take one of his own flock or herd to prepare for the wayfarer who had come to him. . . .'

Then David's anger was greatly kindled against the man; and he said to Nathan, 'As the Lord lives, the man who has done this deserves to die; and he shall restore the lamb fourfold, because he did this thing, and because he had no pity'" (2 Sam. 12:1-6).

When David heard this story, aggression arose in him, but he projected his anger against some one else: "David's anger was greatly kindled *against the man.* . . ." Its inmost cause was the self-condemnation which he repressed.

"Nathan said to David, 'You are the man. . . . Why have you despised the word of the Lord, to do what is evil in his sight?'" . . . The sword of the Word pierced David's heart, striking the sore spot; he admitted his sin. His aggressive condemnation was no longer turned against others, but against himself. "David said to Nathan, 'I have sinned against the Lord.' And Nathan said to David, 'The Lord also has put away your sin; you shall not die.'"

David himself tells about his confession, his admission of his guilt, and of the forgiveness which he received, in Psalms 51 and 32:

"Have mercy on me, O God, according to thy steadfast love; according to thy abundant mercy blot out my transgressions. Wash me thoroughly from my iniquity, and cleanse me from my sin! For I know my transgressions, and my sin is ever before me. Against thee, thee only, have I sinned, and done that which is evil in thy sight, so that thou art justified in thy sentence and blameless in thy judgment" (Ps. 51:1-4).

"Blessed is he whose transgression is forgiven, whose sin is covered. Blessed is the man to whom the Lord imputes no iniquity, and in whose spirit there is no deceit. When I declared not my sin, my body wasted away through my groaning all day long. For day and night thy hand was heavy upon me; my strength was dried up as by the heat of summer. I acknowledged my sin to thee, and I did not hide my iniquity: I said, 'I will confess my transgressions to the Lord'; then thou didst forgive the guilt of my sin" (Ps. 32:1-5).

Deciding to go to confession is not easy for anyone, for inertia as well as conscious opposition within a person plays a part. Pride, self-defense, and fear of men mobilize both reluctance and dislike for exposing one's inner self. And even if we suspect that which we most desire to keep secret is the very thing we ought to confess, yet we often keep silent.

It is useless to force oneself to go to confession. Private confession is, indeed, a private matter; but as such it ought to appeal to our sense of responsibility. For, in the last analysis, we ourselves determine whether we are to obtain the needed help in confession. But that should not prevent us from assisting others by offering them an opportunity to be helped through this means.

In the matter of the opportune time for confession the individual's spiritual and psychic preparedness will, of course, play a part. A boil is opened when ripe for incision.

Often it may take considerable time before confession is made. We have known persons who have been patients in a hospital several times before they have themselves recognized and then disclosed the real cause of their ailment. And more than once we have been approached for soul care counsel only after the patient's dismissal from the hospital, which *then* led to private confession. For a deep regression of sin and guilt creates a deep resistance. Many patients seem to prefer long periods of expensive and often painful treatments to confessing their sin, and they always ask for something that may remove their annoying symptoms, e.g., medication or shock treatments.

But the feeling of guilt which is conditioned on unconfessed sin can not be removed in that way. Such procedure
may be likened to attempts at healing cancer by inducing
hypnosis, or removing an abscess by means of a hypodermic
injection of morphine. Our guilt over against God can be
blotted out only through the declaration of the forgiveness
of sins in the name of Jesus Christ.

In confession we meet problems from all walks and conditions of life. Very frequently they relate to sexual life, to
love relationships, or to marital conditions. The difficulties
may concern untruthfulness, unconciliatory attitude, bitterness, hatred, feeling of guilt because of masturbation, homo-
sexuality, *abortus provocatus,* prevention of conception,
sterilization, etc.

The object of the confessor must not be to rationalize,
explain away, or excuse the guilt confessed by the penitent.
Nor should he treat as a trifle matters which the one making
confession is convinced are sinful. His task is to listen atten-
tively and sympathetically, and his most important commission is to absolve, i.e., to declare the forgiveness of sins.

Even a so-called peccadillo may be enough to fetter the
conscience and to rob one of boldness and joy, as well as to
drain one's psychic energy. I have seen some instances of
what is often considered a trifle (for instance, masturbation),
if unconfessed, may rob a person of assurance of salvation
for years. Many have said during confession, "This is the
first time in my life that I have talked of these things to
somebody else." After confession they have become, as it
were, new men. The pressure of fear has been released; they
were relieved of their burden, and became happy, secure,
satisfied, and free men and women.

Healing in Answer to Prayer. This important and timely
question (often in English termed faith healing) we have

not space in this presentation to discuss fully; but in this connection I want to call attention to the mighty forces of healing with which the prayer of faith connects us, something of which both the Bible and experience testify. Viewing the matter from the point of view of the help here made possible for sufferers, the Church should recognize the great responsibility resting on it in this connection. We have often neglected and failed sick folk by not making use of the tremendous possibilities given us through healing by means of prayer. Many suffering people would have received help if we had utilized the fountains of power laid down in prayer.

Often I have had the pleasure of noting a positive interest in this matter among physicians. I do not readily forget an experience I had along this line some years ago.

A patient at one of our larger hospitals had her ailment diagnosed as an inoperable tumor of the brain, and she was about to be dismissed, as nothing could be done for her at the hospital. But before dismissal she expressed the desire that she be prayed for in accordance with James 5:14. I was sent for, and upon my arrival she told me that she had communicated with her doctor about her desire, as she did not want to have it done without his knowledge. The doctor said that he had no objections to make; on the contrary, he had often wondered, he said, that such procedure was so rarely followed. "If you Christians," he said, "believe in the power of prayer, why do you not practice it more often than you do? I don't understand why." This expression by a physician has often been recalled by me and has been a challenge to me.

The story of the woman has a continuation. Several years afterward, while I was on a lecture tour, a lady who knew the former patient approached me after I was through speaking one evening, and she said that the patient not only was still living, but also had apparently been feeling fine since being prayed for.

Strength to Bear Suffering. There are many who do not get rid of their sickness and suffering, but must endure them the rest of their lives. No one gets by the problem of suffering. It is well known that continued suffering may tempt one to become discouraged, more or less resigned, and bitter. In this situation soul care may be a real help to bring about release, new courage, hope, joy, peace—in brief, to act as a liberating power. Paul did not find it an easy experience with his "thorn in the flesh" (whether this was an organic disease or some other suffering). For this thing he besought the Lord thrice that it might depart from him. His prayer was answered in this wise that he was to keep his infirmity, but, too, that he was to experience the grace of God as a new power in the midst of it. Thus Paul was helped to accept his weakness, not in a spirit of depression and drab resignation, but in faith and renewed hope. From that time forth his weakness ceased to be a hindrance in his spiritual life and in his service, and it was transformed into a channel through which the power of God flowed into his life. "My grace is sufficient for you, for my power is made perfect in weaknesses." He accepted his suffering, thus gaining boldness to say: "I will all the more gladly boast of my weaknesses, that the power of Christ may rest upon me" (2 Cor. 12:9).

There are sick folk who have not in themselves the power to get into contact with the healing and saving forces. There *we* must bring them to the Master (Matt. 9:2), as the suffering often limits the individual's personal sense of responsibility. There are sick and suffering persons who can be held responsible neither for what they do nor for what they omit doing. But that fact does not relieve *us* of responsibility on their behalf; on the contrary, it increases it. We have the responsibility for their getting the help needed, physically, psychically, spiritually. It is indeed the mission of soul care to bring this about. "Bear one another's burdens, and so fulfil the law of Christ" (Gal. 6:2).

Intercession, love, and practical service are powers that bear others to Christ.

In concluding this section I wish to recount two cases of physicians' serving as soul counselors, as these confirm what has been said of the necessity of soul care and of its psychotherapeutic effects.

The first one is told in Dr. Paul Tournier's book *The Bible and Medicine*, the other in Dr. Maeder's *Roads to Psychic Health*.

Dr. Tournier writes:

"One day the wife of a colleague of mine came to Geneva to see me. She said, 'Please help my husband. I do not know just what it is that is distressing him, as he does not unbosom to anyone; but I am of the impression that he is facing a catastrophe. He is worn out nervously. For many years he has not taken a vacation, saying that he cannot afford it, although he works feverishly, from early morning until late night. He sleeps poorly, in spite of taking several sleeping pills every evening. He has neglected his friends, and he devotes no time to me and the children, neither to anyone else, nor to any interest outside of his profession. His life has become a veritable treadmill, and back of his set face I suspect the presence of a terrible, mysterious anguish.'

"And she went on to say, 'Last year he was seriously ill, being hospitalized several months. His doctors were astonished that he reacted so poorly to treatment. Just as if that were strange! After his constant overexertion he was naturally completely worn out. I hoped that his prolonged sickness would have induced him to change his pace, but no; he refused even to take it easier during convalescence, which I begged him to do. He was no sooner out of bed than he once more began his work, more intensely than ever before. If he continues this terrible pace he will have another breakdown.'

"I decided to write my colleague, though wondering greatly whether he would resent my doing so. Would he upbraid his wife for having consulted me? I nervously awaited the outcome.

"But on the contrary, he was pleasant when he came to see me. 'For many years I have thought of looking you up,' he said upon entering my office; 'but I have lacked the courage to do it. Today, however, I have decided to unburden myself completely.'

"And so he disclosed to me the drama of his life. A *faux pas* early in his university days had been followed by others; it is always so in this world that there is an appalling sequence in evil. These lapses had forced him into a veritable prison of loneliness, as he had not dared to unbosom to his wife, nor to his father confessor, a circumstance which increased the accusations of his conscience and also his despair. Losing more and more the control over his passions, he drifted steadily into new compromises. 'All day long,' he said, 'I am giving wholesome counsel to my patients, since I believe that the art of healing consists as much in reconstituting misspent lives as in prescribing curative medicine, while I myself know what I must do to regain health and peace of mind, but I am unable to do it.'

"His moral lapses had also involved him in economic difficulties, which he was anxious to hide from his wife, whose fortune he had dissipated. He constantly hoped to clear up his straitened circumstances by working night and day, but his debts grew apace, as he felt constrained to keep his fees lower than the time spent on his patients warranted. This inclination toward benevolence is known to have its source in an inferiority complex; his attempts at thus doing good constituted a kind of self-sacrificing act by way of restitution, an atonement for guilt, and also a form of escapism.

"He also told of his hospitalization. A tiny local infection had rapidly developed into a serious case of blood poisoning, something which had not surprised him, as he had long expected a catastrophe. His illness had a definite meaning to him: as an inescapable day of reckoning. Perhaps, he thought, it was sent him by fate to give him a chance of liberating himself since it had perforce put a stop to the devilish sequence by which he had allowed himself to be driven along. But, would he be able to make use of this chance?

"The deep meaning of the illness, the reproaches he could not get rid of, the decisions which he so often made, but which he doubted he could carry through more successfully in the future—all these swirled in his mind during his attacks of fever. He would so gladly have confided in the doctors! Were they not his dear friends, eagerly anxious to help him? The head doctor, an eminent physician, in whom he really had complete confidence, dealt with him most devotedly; and, recognizing fully the psychologic significance in the treatment, he never neglected to say a word of encouragement to his patient.

"But the reader will understand that something wholly different was buried beneath the surface. The patient had a secret so intimate, so pressing, that the professor with his cortege of assistant physicians daily had to leave his bed without the patient having become their confidant. Every day the doctors conversed about blood cultures which stubbornly remained sterile, something that was a puzzling problem to these learned men, as was also the infection's resistance to antibiotics. How could they, without direct provocation, proceed to discuss the very different problems burdening the patient's soul?

"I knew that my colleague was a Christian believer, and that induced me to inquire whether his faith, his church, could not have helped him. At that he said, 'Indeed, there you touch the most tragic aspect of my whole situation. I am thought of as an active Catholic, yet for years I have stayed away from confession and communion. Earlier I was greatly attached to my father confessor, in whom I had full confidence; but he was moved to another city, and I did not have the courage to apply to another priest. Now I suffer greatly under the realization that there is a huge difference between my reputation and the life I am really leading, a circumstance that is sapping still further the strength of my spirit. As the years have passed it has become increasingly difficult for me to resume the practice of my religion—for me who am regarded by everybody as a good Catholic! This anomaly, too, was ever in my thoughts while I was a patient, and I promised myself to take the decisive step. But I could not do it!'

"Often I have been thinking about that hospital experience of my friend; of the tragedy which the professor's daily visits actually was to him; of the spiritual loneliness his patient really felt in spite of all the kindness shown him; of the impossible conversations which ensued on two so essentially different planes—and I realized that if the doctor busies himself only with purely scientific matters and thinks only of microbes, chemical doses, or psychic complexes, then his patient will never get to unburden himself to him of the problems which harass him, and which deal with the *meaning*, not the mechanism, of his illness.

"But, back to the story of my friend and to his visit with me. He got through with his disclosures. I said nothing, for I had nothing to say. In the matter of science we are called on to instruct, to advise, to order; but in things of the spirit we can only listen, understand, love, and *pray*. The answer must come from God. After a long silence my friend began to say aloud the things God gave him to say. Simply, but clearly he enumerated the things necessary for him to do if order and obedience were to be restored in his life. I limited my remarks to point out certain items in areas where I knew such questions would be of assistance to him. At last I said, 'That letter which you will write, *when* do you mean to write it?' He answered, 'As soon as I get home.'

"Some months later he wrote me a letter which moved me greatly. It was a paean of praise to God for grace received. He had carried through the program that he had enumerated in my office.

"He had resumed going to confession and to communion. He had confided in his wife. Together they had planned the vacation now fully decided on. And they looked forward to their vacation journey as to a second honeymoon travel."

Dr. Maeder writes:

"I shall now tell, from my personal experience, about a case which can only be characterized as one of soul care, because it illustrates the possibility of giving effective help of the kind which ordinarily should not be given in a doctor's case. Once I received a telephone call from a former schoolmate of mine whom I had not seen for more than 35 years. His name was Hans. What he said was a veritable SOS call: —'I have for more than five years suffered from Parkinson's disease (a serious illness of the central nervous system, with tremors and weakness of the muscles). I have tried all possible medical help, but have only grown worse. Give me a wholly new medicine; otherwise I have no other recourse but suicide.'—This he told me with great difficulty, in a stuttering voice. It was very hard for me to hear and understand what he said, not only because of his speech difficulties, but also because of the poor man's very evident emotional tenseness.

"I knew that we here were up against a very difficult case. The following day I called on Hans. He sat in an armchair; he was practically unable to rise; his face looked stark and expressionless. He appeared worn and exhausted, strongly marked by his illness and his hard fate, presenting indeed a shocking sight. In a faltering, lisping voice, at times impossible to understand, he asked me at once whether I had brought the new medicine.

"As a doctor I saw at once that medical aid would here be unavailing; his sickness is generally regarded as incurable, and he had already tried all thinkable means. It was equally clear to me that chances for obtaining aid through psychologic treatments were small indeed, especially as conversation would be very difficult. Besides, he was interested in only one thing: whether there still existed a means of healing for him. As he stared at me, desperate and suspicious, I suddenly found myself saying, stressing every word: 'Yes, I have the remedy with me, but you can scarcely get it at a drug store; I bring you a message from Jesus Christ.' Greatly to my own surprise these were the words that came over my lips, as of their own accord. He looked at me in great bewilderment; he did not know what to say or do, but he evidently was interested.

"I then proceeded to say, without having had any communication from him, that his worst illness just then was his despair, his violent excitement on account of all his suffering.

He seemed, I said, greatly irritated both by his fellow men and by everything in connection with himself; he was evidently a great trial to his family—that was my immediate impression when, upon entering the house, I had spent a few moments with him in the presence of his greatly worried wife. In this serious agony of soul Jesus Christ could be the only helper. As physicians had tried in vain to relieve his bodily suffering, it was clear that they could do nothing further for him in that respect.

"He looked astonished at me, but not in disapproval, on the contrary, he seemed willing to listen. And presently he admitted that he actually was as difficult to deal with for his wife and children as he was disgusted with himself. After a while he admitted, too, that there was at least one bright spot in his existence: He had no financial worries, and the family could live comfortably on saved-up capital and investments. Likewise he acknowledged that he had a good wife, who nursed him and also otherwise gave him good care, while many other women doubtless would have resented having so sick and helpless a husband and in some way would have sought compensation for an unpleasant situation. —I offered to see him once a week, not as a doctor but as a friend, an offer which he accepted gladly.

"I shall not tell in detail about the interviews which we subsequently had, nor about the experiences we had jointly. But he learned gradually to unburden himself in prayer, to be less critical of his family, and to be grateful for such blessings which he still had. The Bible got to mean a good deal to him, giving him comfort and strength. My visits seemed to please him much, his face actually beaming when he saw me. The turn for the better in his spiritual life worked also, in course of time, a change for the better in his physical and psychic condition. He slept better, and could at length dismiss the attendant who had been needed for quite some time. Bodily he became less helpless, even more mobile. He who long had been unable to leave his chair became for some time strong enough not only to get up, but also to walk down the stairs with me and out on the street.

"This improvement in his bodily condition may be taken as an illustration of the impression that in the case of chronic physical suffering the patient's spiritual attitude is an important factor either in easing or in making worse his entire condition. At any rate, the positive influence was in this case astonishingly great and gratifying. In spite of what I said to him about the nature of his illness, Hans was all the time convinced that he might get well. During the following year he twice went abroad for the purpose of undergoing a cure-treatment at a sanatorium specializing in treating Parkinson's disease. The second attempt did not turn out well. The hyoscyamine-treatment used (with a Bulgarian root) caused, after a time, a poisoning which, together with other complications, led to his death.

"It is instructive for us physicians, particularly for us psychotherapists, to observe how a pure soul care may have ameliorating, informative, and strengthening results also in cases of serious bodily and psychic need. By the use of only spiritual means very essential results are obtained, for the benefit both of the patient and his family. Thus there are also other means and resources than those given us physicians, a means *sui generis* (of its own kind) which is fully warrantable beside our medical practice. This means not only an enlargement of our knowledge, but it gives us, too, a further reason for tolerance and for willingness to co-operate with soul counselors. The experience told of above was just as valuable and enriching to me as it proved to be to my sick former schoolmate."

Chapter IX

The Significance of Personality

Earlier we have touched on the significance of contact for the ultimate success of soul care and of psychotherapy. And, if contact is to become an effective means, a mutual correspondence in the contactual relation must be presupposed. The bridge between the two parties—doctor and patient; pastor and confider or patient—must be passable, in such a way as to make mutual understanding possible.

Consequently, contact must be geared for cooperation, and cooperation must be built on interdependence and mutual responsibility. A heavy responsibility rests on him who is to be of assistance to others, a responsibility of being willing to make decisions and to devise measures for the benefit of the patient. But the responsibility is a joint one, as the aim is to assist the patient himself to make decisions for which he is ready to assume the responsibility. Responsibility is an expression of the high, eternal worth of personality. No real service is done a person by relieving him of a responsibility which he himself should feel and carry. It is much better to *appeal* to his sense of responsibility and thus awaken this sense, than to carry the full responsibility for him.

A contact relation often creates many problems, some of which have connection with a want on the part of the patient in ability to establish contact. A discussion of these problems lies outside the scope of this book; they are, however, discussed in textbooks on psychiatry and soul care, to which the interested reader is referred.

But the reason back of insufficient contact and of serious conflict situations and problems may also be found with the pastor or with the physician. We have earlier pointed out that contact is established through a *reciprocal* relation. The personal problem of the patient is also a personal challenge to the soul counselor. Hence, our *personality* plays a decisive role in the contact relation.

This is strongly underscored by psychotherapists. Thus Professor Dr. Gabriel Langfeldt says in his book *Nervous Sufferings:*

"High qualifications ought to be demanded of those seeking authorization as analysts, not only from the point of view of theoretical and practical education, but also from the point of view of *personality,* a demand, however, that is difficult, if not impossible, to meet. If the analyst himself is a person of complexes he will not, as a matter-of-course, be able to help his patient. On the contrary, he may become, on account of a one-sided attitude toward his own complexes, a serious danger, as there would be no way to control his activity."

Dr. Arne Kanter dealt with the significance of personality in a recent lecture to physicians on psychotherapeutic methods, saying: "Also in psychotherapy several ways lead to the goal. In the last analysis, method may, perhaps, not be the most essential, but rather the personal qualifications of the therapist. Method is indeed an effective instrument when used by a gifted person; but in the hand of a gifted person the work might, perhaps, be equally effective through the use of *other* instruments."

Personality is insolubly bound to the treatment tried on the patient. Dr. A. Maeder says in his work: *Roads to Psychic Health:*

"We psychiatrists must exercise strict self-control. Even as it is a mistake to use non-sterile instruments in an operation, so our personal behavior may be justly rebuked if we practice psychotherapy in an unclear frame of mind, full of complexes, and without clear perception of the core of things. Practice is doubtless more difficult for us than for the surgeon because our own person is part of our instrumental equipment. Our attitude toward our work may be likened to that of a singer, whose instrument is his own voice."

If personality is a part of the instrumental equipment of psychotherapy, this is no less the case in soul care. The personality of the soul counselor ought to be an instrument and a tool for God unto service of his fellow men.

The crucial question then gets to be what it is which makes our personality a contact-creating one. By way of an answer many important factors may be pointed out as contributing to the upbuilding and development of personality. Here may be mentioned that the ability to create contact is related to the natural psychic and bodily equipment, to innate abilities and aptitudes, to scholarship, education, and experience. On the other hand it should be mentioned that many are hampered by heredity, constitution, *milieu*, weakness, and illness.

It must be freely admitted that these factors play a large part in the matter of establishing contact, both positively and negatively, but with this admission made not all is said in regard to the contact relation. As stated earlier, there is in existence something irrational, something inexplicable, something that cannot be thoroughly explored by scientific methods. It is impossible to prescribe beforehand how a personal contact is to be established, since it *may* be brought about contrary to our schemes, rules, methods, known facts, ideas, and experiences. At times it is done spontaneously, through intuition and inspiration, at other times by the very use of our reason and our knowledge. Very often indeed our feelings and preconceived notions have given us a wrong lead and have brought us far afield. And the result turned out to be complications and conflicts instead of contact. It was not until afterwards that we saw that we should have prepared the situation quite differently, both psychically and spiritually, and we should have taken time for more exhaustive investigation. To know *how* is both important and necessary.

But experience shows that it is possible to have extensive knowledge of both the Bible and of human nature, besides the very best theological, medical, psychiatric, and psychological training, and yet lack the ability to create contact. The reason for this is found in the fact that personal contact is not primarily created by what we know, nor by what we say, not even by what we do. Of greater importance than what we know, say, and do, is what we *are*, as contact is an existential matter and is established by what we are. It must be a *personal* contact, and that is born *"in der Begegnung"* (in the process of meeting) when the *I* meets the *you*. It takes place when man meets fellow man, when two souls encounter each other, when a person finds another person. Then is created a human, psychic contact which is the prerequisite for a deeper spiritual contact.

It is not possible to formulate definite rules and to draw

schemata for establishing such a contact. Experience, like life, seeks it own channels and follows a procedure not easy to describe.

However, there is another matter which may be, and should be, noted: If personal contact is to be made, personal requirements must also be present in order to make contact at all possible. We shall, therefore, mention some of the requirements which are of such a decisive importance for the establishing of contact. The requirements here mentioned are such as apply chiefly to soul counselors, although they may apply, at least in part, also to the personality of a psychotherapist.

Listening in Silence

In sermonizing the preacher speaks while his hearers listen in silence. In soul care the opposite is often the case. Here the pastor must learn the art of listening in silence and of letting the other person speak—speak out about what is on his mind; for in personal soul care listening is even more important for the pastor than speaking. Many persons are in need of a chance to speak out, to open their hearts completely. This is often a necessary condition for receiving help, bodily, psychic, and spiritual. But they will open up only to one in whom they have confidence, to one taking plenty of time to listen to what they have to say. The counselor must endeavor by all means to understand how to let them talk freely of their distresses, without prejudice on his part.

To take time to listen to a man is often the same as to give him the help he is in need of.

Listening in silence produces a feeling of quietude. And

quietude gives rise to clarity and concentration about that which is at the heart of the actual situation for those seeking help. It gets to be like a mirror for seeing and rediscovering oneself, a help to see one's problems in a new light and also to solve them. It is like emerging into the light and warmth of a sunny day. That which was frozen within one melts, the shackled one is loosed

But listening in silence does not mean being passive, nor neutral. On the contrary, one gets to feel in touch with a fellow being's need as, by listening, one enters into his very condition and shares his experiences. To listen in this way requires both patience and endurance, in order that one may be prepared for the "tiresome" pauses, which, by the way, are the most wearing part of the experience.

However, listening in silence means more than taking time, having time, and giving time to listen to another. The reason is that our own mind, our personal attitude, is involved. To listen well we must have peace and repose within. The other person will readily feel a spirit of restlessness on our part. Better five minutes with peace within than a half-hour given in restlessness. Not a mind scattered and divided, but a mind calm and collected is the one able to listen well. Jesus advised entering into one's closet, shutting the door, and then praying to the Father in secret. A soul counselor must first of all learn to be still before the Lord. And to the extent that he is just that, and obedient to Christ, will he be able to listen in silence to his fellow men's needs and to give them help at the right time. For a pastor the Greek word *kairos* (in the Bible: in due season) is a key word that will open locked doors.

During such a listening service the most important part is not having the ability to understand all of that which is said, nor to interpret correctly all the psychic reactions involved, not even trying to solve all the problems presented, but simply to listen sympathetically. For finding a fellow man willing and able to listen to one's woes is like getting rest after a long and tiring march.

A man had conceived the idea of seeking spiritual help in a foreign country; but the pastor to whom he applied did not know the stranger's language. But he did know how to listen. When the foreigner had talked a long time—the pastor silently listening—he suddenly felt released; for while the pastor had been listening and *praying*, the cause of his difficulty had become clear to the visitor, and he also realized where help and strength were to be had. And so he returned to his own country a new man.

The necessity of listening in silence cannot be overemphasized as a prerequisite for achieving contact. Some have deemed it so important that they have devised certain methods for making it more effective. Some of this is encountered, for instance, in Carl Rogers' theses about "nondirective counseling."

The fundamental principle of this counseling process is expressed by Rogers: "Effective counseling consists in a certain organized, permissive condition allowing the patient to arrive at an understanding of himself, which will enable him to take a positive step in the light of this new orientation." (From E. Anker-Nilsen's book *New Ways in Soul Care*, p. 224.)

This method of Rogers points out many valuable things which may be made use of in soul care. But care should be taken in making use of ready-made psychological and psychotherapeutic methods in the giving of soul care, as soul care must not become a method of treatment, but always remain a personalized care of an individual. This care is not to be a treatment of cases, but an understanding, sympathetic help given an individual brother man in a concrete, actual situation of need.

Tact and Discretion

There is a shyness of soul which demands due respect. Just as unnatural as it is to expose one's body in public, so it is to lay bare one's inner life within hearing of many. This shyness is a safeguard around personality; it is a part of our independence and also of maintaining it. For a person to attach himself to almost anybody for the sake of making disclosures of the most intimate relations is not a good sign.

This reserve or modesty is a criterion of sound psychic reactions. To know one another is not the same as to know everything about one another. We had better be resigned to the fact that in another person's being there is something hidden from us, something which is and should remain a secret. Within every man's soul there is something inscrutable, something unfathomable. The depth of my fellow man's personality I shall never be able to know fully because I have no means of sounding it.

The Bible tells us that this is so because we are eternal beings. "Also he has put eternity into man's mind, yet so that he cannot find out what God has done from the beginning to the end" (Eccl. 3:11).

We must not forget that we are created by God. And that which God has created is so valuable as to defy all our attempts at estimation. Jesus put it thus: "For what will it profit a man, if he gains the whole world and forfeits his life? Or what shall a man give in return for his life?" (Matt. 16:26).

We must therefore entertain respect, esteem, even reverence for the human soul. This reverence places bounds which must suffer no trespass. "I have been increasingly convinced of the significance of this reverence" (Albert Schweitzer).

There is something inconceivably great about the inmost life of another person.

Our anthropologic view is determinative for our manner of helping our fellow men. It is, therefore, no indifferent matter whether we regard man as a rational or a nonrational being (the terms rational and nonrational being here used in their philosophic sense: as capable of being thoroughly understood, or not, by man's reason). A view of life which looks upon man as a rational being (in this sense) lowers man to the level of a mechanism; i.e., something which can be fully understood by reason. It is precisely the irrational and inscrutable about man which creates wonder and reverence.

We have no inherent right to invade the inmost soul life of another person; and every one has a right to turn away from an inquisitive, officious counselor. Respect for psychic reserve will help us to follow the right procedure in giving soul care; such an attitude will be no real hindrance in establishing contact. For every contact presupposes both a certain distance as well as a certain intimacy. (See page 133).

This tension creates both discretion and delicacy of touch. It is better to be a bit too reserved than too forward. Rather a step behind than two beyond the limit. Many are rather wary in spiritual matters. Wanting deference and respect may close a door which otherwise would have opened. But awaiting patiently the seasonable time will create a feeling of security and confidence. We must enroll in the school of the Master and learn of him. Note, for instance, how he dealt with the woman of Samaria. He spoke to her quietly and naturally about things that caught her interest.

Psychic reserve tells us that the best contact is established when one is *alone* with another. If there are several present, e.g., at a party, and two persons want a *tete-a-tete* conversation, they usually look for a quiet corner before they begin their exchange of thoughts. It is therefore difficult to talk in a personal way to a patient in a hospital ward, where there usually are several beds. It feels unnatural to exchange confidences when others are likely to hear what is said. Most people react in a truer manner *tete-a-tete* than in a gathering.

In a hospital ward lay thirteen men. As the chaplain called on them, going from bed to bed, he found that their attitude toward Christianity varied. One especially expressed rather clearly that he was negatively inclined, and he also tried to influence some of the others to take a similar attitude. After listening awhile the chaplain said upon leaving, "A time may come when you, too, will be in need of Jesus Christ."

Some days later the chaplain met that young man in the corridor and greeted him. The man stopped and said, "May I talk to you alone, pastor?" When they were alone the patient said, "I want so much to become a Christian, but how am I to go about it?"—The incident proved that the contact which could not be established in the presence of others, was brought about *tete-a-tete*.

I am also thinking of the many opportunities for personal contact offered by divine services, social gatherings, meetings, etc. Such chances at "after meetings" should be made use of. Oftentimes contact is hindered because no room for counseling together alone may be available. Rooms for counseling and prayer should be provided in every church. And arrangements should be made for obtaining the necessary quiet and privacy.

During a series of meetings we invited people who desired counseling to remain after the service. Besides the large meeting hall there was only a rather small room available, and that was soon filled. One of the men I talked to said, "I feel that I cannot say what is on my heart where others can hear me." As I understood his reaction very well we agreed to meet at another time and place.

Psychic shyness may also express itself as real bashfulness. But there is, too, a bashfulness which is a cloak for cowardice or for personal ambition. Bashful persons are usually unable to ask for assistance, but that does not mean that they do not need it, nor that they may not really want it. Perhaps they are even waiting for it, but are too timid to ask for it. They are in need of a personal invitation by way of encouragement, a bit of aid, a "push." A suggestion as to a later interview may be in order. Perhaps they may be in need of several such, but as they are too bashful to request them, they need assistance. Soul counselors are in need of the mind of Christ, who came "to seek and to save the lost" (Luke 19:10).

But reserve of soul does not exempt the individual from responsibility. The counselor is to withdraw to the extent that the penitent may make his own decision. Responsibility is an expression for the high worth of personality. One of the objectives of soul care is to assist in making clear to a man that he is responsible for the kind of life he is leading. Responsibility and freedom belong together; it is as the Danish writer Kaj Munk wrote in his "Foraaret saa sagte kommer" (Spring Is Late in Arriving): "—he felt that he had come into freedom, the best of all freedoms: the one called responsibility."

We must guard against exposing a man to spiritual pressure. No one can by human power be coerced into heaven. But we have the responsibility of giving our fellow men the opportunity of choosing God's way and salvation.

Spiritual reserve must not prevent us from presenting the truth; this can be done more readily face to face than in a crowd, even as Jesus presented it to Nicodemus when they were alone together at night: "Unless one is born anew, he cannot see the kingdom of God" (John 3:3). Or as He did to the woman of Samaria, in such a way that she was led to know the truth and to acknowledge it, thus giving her the help and salvation she was in need of.

Naturalness

We must seek to establish contact with our neighbor in a natural way. But, as that which is natural for one may be unnatural for another, we must guard against copying others, even if it seems to us that they succeed better than we do.

In order to be natural we must be able to accept ourselves just as we really are. But the prerequisite for this is learning to know ourselves, to find ourselves. Which, indeed, is a difficult and slowly acquired art.

Psychologic literature frequently calls attention to the term personality as a derivative of the Latin *persona*, which originally meant a mask used by actors in Roman theaters. The mask was a "false aspect," as it did not show the actor's real face, but represented the part which he was playing.

Similarly our manner of being (character) is often a mask put on in our association with others. "The clergyman's unction, the physician's professional manner at the sickbed, the lawyer's wise mien, the saleswoman's jaunty *jargon,* are, all of them, indications of signs of weakness resorted to in order to cover the poverty of the real self" (Hadfield).

We readily put on a mask to hide, as it were, both from others and from ourselves, pretending to be something different from what we are. Just call to mind how concerned we are about what other people think of us; their favor, esteem, and opinion mean a great deal to us. Taken all in all, our relation to "other people" is a decisive factor in our lives; and fear of man is a tremendous power.

In this connection mention should be made of evaluating oneself wrongly: either overestimation, caused by arrogance and pride, or underestimation, emanating from depression. Wrong evaluation of self may show itself in various ways. Self-assertion is displayed as faultfinding, captiousness, and self-righteousness. It is easy to see the faults of others, but hard indeed to be aware of one's own. "Why do you see the speck that is in your brother's eye, but do not notice the log that is in your own eye?" (Matt. 7:3).

This attitude leads into a wrong relation to oneself. It is true that there is such a thing as a positive ambition which spurs a person on to achievement, but there is also an ambition which is wholly egocentric, resulting in self-seeking, self-love, and in pitying oneself.

How, then, are we to get away from egotism and learn to evaluate ourselves more sanely?

Jesus said, "You shall love your neighbor as *yourself*" (Matt. 22:39). We are rather given to stress the duty of loving our neighbor, but we often leave out the last part of the

sentence, as *yourself,* thus overlooking that there *is* a commandment enjoining love of self. This true love of self is
found in the hearts of those who truly love God; and this
kind of self-love saves us on the one hand from despondency
and self-depreciation, on the other from arrogance and self-
seeking.

The Bible tells us how we may get this true perspective
of self, so that we may find ourselves and accept ourselves
as we really are. Thus it is told of the prodigal son (Luke 15:
11-24) that *"he came to himself."* He learned to see his sin
and to acknowledge it: "Father, I have sinned against
heaven, and before you." This was not merely a purpose;
it was a *decision* leading to action.

Very likely the lad, while homeward bound, was fearful
of not being received by his father. But it turned out that
the father not only received him, but that he was more
anxious to accept and forgive him than the son was to get
home to confess his sin. Before he got to confess a single
thing he was in his father's arms.

Since this is the way in which God receives us, we dare
to recognize ourselves, our imperfections and our sins.

When God is willing to save me and to make use of me
in his service, even as I am, then I have no right to despise
and underestimate myself. Him whom Jesus loved and gave
his life for, I, too, shall love. Thus, I am to love both my
neighbor and myself. This feeling gives me both the right
kind of meekness and the right kind of boldness, resulting in
a genuine and true evaluation of self.

Genuineness

Personal contact presupposes a relation of confidence; and
confidence is engendered by the genuineness shining forth

from the personality of the soul counselor or the psycho-therapist. Back of that which we are endeavoring to impart to others there must be a personal conviction. The truth of the theory presented must be corroborated and exemplified in one's life and practice. A counselor can establish no spir-itual contact if sincerity and genuineness are lacking in his own spiritual life. A patient will soon perceive whether the pastor personally believes and is interested in that which he tells others.

Fair, sober criticism may frequently be needed to keep us awake psychically and spiritually. This kind of a spir-itual arouser we meet in the writings of the Danish philoso-pher Søren Kierkegaard. They contain a caustic, biting cri-ticism of "Christendom," his appellation for "official Chris-tianity"; but the ethical seriousness which motivates the author's criticisms is not easily forgotten. His main thesis is that only he who unconditionally lets the demands of God govern his life is able to experience truth. The question then gets to be whether we are willing to accept the consequences of these demands.

It follows that it is by the confrontation with the con-sequences that "Christendom" most easily is arrested. It is by the confrontation of the practical consequences of modern Christianity with those of pristine Christianity that the dif-ference between the two clearly appears. In this connection suffice it to call to mind how the author has a predilection for comparing "Christendom" with "contemporaneousness" (in Danish: *Samtidighed,* a favorite term of Kierkegaard's). "By the fact that Christendom is placed in the situation of contemporaneousness the former is exposed and judged; and that which renders the relation plain is just the practical consequences of Christianity" (Dr. Per Lønning's *Samtidighetens situasjon,* pp. 183-184)

This tension relationship led Søren Kierkegaard into deep, serious crises, in order that he might gain a clear perspective of himself. A characteristic expression of this experience he has given in his so-called *Gilleleje* Memorandum of 1835: "That which I am really lacking in my case is a clear realization of *what I shall do, . . .*" (Finn Jor: *Søren Kierkegaard,* pp. 27-28).

Soul care is concerned not only with pure doctrine and the right message. Experience has demonstrated that the personal spiritual potency of the counselor is decisive for the penetrative power of soul care. Of Stephen Scripture says, "But they could not withstand the wisdom and the Spirit with which he spoke" (Acts 6:10)

Clear, logical arguments and dogmatic formulations do not suffice; dynamics of spirit and genuineness of faith must permeate the whole presentation.

Bishop J. C. Heuch tells in one of his books about a young pastor who called on an old, sick lady who had never shown any interest in religion. Now that she was very sick and apparently approaching death the pastor felt it to be his duty to try to awaken in her an interest in salvation. He was courteously received, but when he broached the subject of her soul's welfare she said:

"If you will first answer a question of mine you may talk to me freely and at length about religion. Do you yourself believe that which you desire me to believe? Could you testify to its truth with your dying breath?"

The young pastor was embarrassed, as he was not sure that he had such a faith, and he therefore said evasively, "It should not matter to you whether *I* believe or not; it is not my faith that will save you, but the message which I bring."

But then the aged lady sat up in bed and said scornfully, "Begone! Don't prate to me about a faith in which you don't believe. But upon leaving take this piece of advice with you: Remember that a room where death is in the offing is no place for play acting; for you are acting a part, nothing else."

He wanted to expostulate, but as her finger pointed peremptorily toward the door, he had no choice but to leave, humiliated as never before in his life.

We cannot point out the way to others if we ourselves are not on the way. If I am to bring others into contact with God I myself must have such a contact. Religious phrases will do no good. The very best methods will prove unavailing. Routine and habit are danger shoals in soul care. Correspondence of life to doctrine is the most convincing proof of the truth of the Christian mesage. "A genuine Christian is worth more than a hundred volumes full of so-called proofs of the truth of the Christian faith" (Lavater).

Being charged with the responsibility of helping others is the most insistent challenge to ourselves, as it confronts us with a call to self-examination. Many are the temptations and dangers lying in ambush for the Christian. Among the most dangerous of these highwaymen is deceit of self. In the seven letters to churches in Revelation 2 and 3 there are frequent warnings: "You have the name of being alive, and you are dead." "So, because you are lukewarm, and neither cold nor hot, I will spew you out of my mouth." "But I have this against you, that you have abandoned the love you had at first."

The greatest danger in such a state of mind is that the

facade and all outward manifestations are in order, and that one is accounted a Christian by others. But Christ, who reads the heart, knows what is lacking, and also what is needed. In the Word he tells us clearly how he can and will help us. Again and again he says, "Repent." We are so prone to think of conversion as a one-time act, and to forget that once converted does not mean that there is no more need of repentance and conversion.

The spiritual life's genuineness is preserved only through daily repentance and renewal. This involves self-examination, but it also binds us to Christ, saves us from self-deception, and keeps us spiritually awake. Examining oneself gets to be a necessary cleansing process in order that Christ may dwell in us, to accomplish his work for us and with us. In Jeremiah 15:19 we read:

"If you return, I will restore you, and you shall stand before me. If you utter what is precious, and not what is worthless, you shall be as my mouth."

Also about daily renewal the Bible speaks solemn words of warning: "Do not be conformed to this world but be transformed by the renewal of your mind, that you may prove what is the will of God, what is good and acceptable and perfect" (Rom. 12:2).

A life that is not renewed dies. Consequently, daily renewal belongs in the genuine spiritual life. "So we do not lose heart. Though our outer nature is wasting away, our inner nature is being renewed every day" (2 Cor. 4:16).

On this point many experience great difficulties, and are tempted to become discouraged. Expressions such as these are heard: "I am so unready; everything is in a tangle for me."—"I fall far short in so many ways; how then may I even try to be of help to others?"—"I am so often in doubt about my own relation to God."

Can God use us even so?

By way of answer I shall tell something which has been a real help to me. I am thinking of experiences at deathbeds of Christian believers, some of them men or women of high repute among the brethren. At the close of a good, brotherly conversation I have usually asked what passages of the Bible they would want me to read to them. Then I have always noted that they would name some passage telling about Jesus as the Savior of sinners, as the justifier of the ungodly; *that* to them was the dearest they knew. Eyes would shine and hearts beat in thanksgiving when I would read about the prodigal son, about the robber on the cross, about the publican in the temple; such passages as John 3:16; 6:37; 1 John 1:7-9; Isa. 43:1 and 25; 53-5.—The learned scientist must often resort to the plainest gospel declarations, even as the most unsophisticated layman.

A genuine Christian will never on earth be able to say that he has no sin (1 John 1:8). The day when he feels that he is definitely through with sin, that day he is through with Christ. Only as long as we live in constant confession of sin, are we in possession of forgiveness of sin (1 John 1:7 and 9).

But, the consciousness and acknowledgment of incompleteness, unworthiness, impotence, frailty, sin and guilt do not render us unfit for the service of God. It was while feeling the most despondent about his own unworthiness that Peter was called to be a fisher of men. In answer to his, "Depart from me, for I am a sinful man, O Lord," Jesus said. "Do not be afraid; henceforth you will be catching men" (Luke 5:8 and 10).

It does not primarily depend on our achievements nor upon our words and utterances, whether we may be used by God. Not so much *what* you say as *how* you say it, will win souls unto God.

In our day-by-day endeavors we shall doubtless be guilty of foolish actions, of errors, and of sins; and very often we shall act unwisely. But if we are sincere and genuine, these are not the worst sins of which we may be guilty. When we are weak, then we are strong (2 Cor. 12:10); for then God can use us.

Love

Love is an absolute prerequisite for service in God's kingdom in accordance with his will. Without it our work is vain even though it may consist in the most self-sacrificial deeds. The Word of God declares that without love our words and our services are profitless. (See 1 Cor. 13; John 21:15-16; 2 Cor. 5:14.)

Love will open locked doors and pierce every hindrance. It seeks contact until it finds it. For "love bears all things, believes all things, hopes all things, endures all things." It looks through all screens, all kinds of *camouflage*, all the way into the core of things. And in every human being it sees a message—a gift—from God.

Love opens our eyes to the intrinsic worth of every personality, whether poor or rich, young or old, impossible and ill-disposed or kind and tractable. It espies the soul in the tramp, the criminal, the idiot, the incurably insane—in everybody. Therefore it is able to do that which mere human power cannot do.

Christian love is something more than kind feelings, more than sympathy. For good feelings alone have not the power to liberate from antipathy, bitterness, and hatred. But love has, for love is of God.

Christian love reaches out even to persons who impress us unfavorably. Jesus says that love embraces also one's enemies. "Love your enemies and pray for those who persecute you" (Matt. 5:44).

Love can change a person's entire life, lead him from darkness into light, from despair to hope. It can, really, render the impossible possible.

A pastor has told an experience which he had in his work among prisoners shortly after Norway's liberation in 1945. One of the problems which he was facing was that of getting contact established between the prisoners and himself, for he realized that without this contact both his preaching and his soul care would largely be in vain.

When he returned to the prison after a three weeks' vacation he felt that such contact which had been effected, in some way had been broken. His first service after his return was held outdoors. He introduced his sermon with a few personal remarks: "During my absence you have been constantly in my thoughts and in my prayers. And I should like to tell you plainly what my feelings toward you have been: in my prayers for you I have felt a strong *love* for you"— after which he went on with his sermon, feeling that the broken contact had been reestablished. And after that he had so many calls for personal pastoral care that he found it difficult to arrange time for them.

Not long afterwards one of the prisoners sought him out and told the following about himself. When he was brought to the prison he felt himself definitely through with church, pastors, and Christianity. Psychically he was greatly depressed, a condition which steadily grew worse, until he felt strongly tempted to commit suicide. That first Sunday after the chaplain's return he was listlessly walking about in the prison yard. All of a sudden he heard hymn singing. As he walked in that direction he noticed a large group of men. As he stopped irresolutely he heard the pastor's introductory remarks. They arrested him, and he stayed through the service, during which a wonderful thing happened, one that he described in this way:

"Instead of committing suicide I gave my life to God that day."

In this way a contact established through love may bring about a complete change in a person's life.

Many could indeed have been helped into contact with the gospel if they had met the love of Christ in some fellow man. Christians need the experience of Paul expressed in 2 Cor. 5:14: "For the love of Christ controls us."

But love is not identical with indulgent yielding. The love of God has in it an element of judgment. The example of Jesus showed love toward the sinner, but also hatred of sin. His love was compassion for the sinner, but also a judgment on uncharitableness, falsehood, and unrighteousness.

The late Bishop Berggrav of Oslo has an arresting story of this judgment of love in his book *The Soul of the Prisoner, and Our Own:*

"A man in his thirties, with a considerable prison record, was one day reported to me as being particularly depressed and agitated. He had just received one of the very fine letters which his mother regularly sent him, and which he also was in the habit of answering in a filial way. He paced up and down in his cell when I entered. He seemed in a truculent mood even though we generally were on friendly terms.

" 'What is wrong?'

" '*I have received sentence.*'

" 'Who has sentenced you?'

" 'Never mind! *I am sentenced.* I care nothing about the sentences of judges; I defy the magistrates; I care nothing about the judgment of you prison authorities—not yours either, Pastor!'

"I interrupted: 'You ought to know very well that we in this prison *judge* no one. In our eyes you are human beings. We are not here as judges, but as helpers.'

" 'I know that. But even if you did judge me I'd care nothing about it—not even if God did.'

" 'But tell me, man, what has made you so unhappy: *Who* has passed sentence on you?'

" 'Mother, mother!' He fairly shouted the words, pressing his hands against his temples—'*Mother has judged me!*'

" 'Your mother? But, man, I have read the letters you receive from her, also this last one; and more loving letters simply do not exist.'

" 'That's just it! If she only had said: I'll never want to see you again, you who have laid my life waste, broken my hopes, made me prematurely gray, exhausted my supply of tears! If she only had disowned me! *But she loves me!* She will not give me up.—Oh, mother has judged me!' "

He broke down, something which he did not otherwise easily do. But an hour later the pastor left the cell, a wiser and more understanding man, having learned more about the judgment contained in pure, unselfish, sacrificing love than any course in theology had ever taught him. "And this is the judgment, that the light has come into the world" (John 3:19). That light is love. And pure love contains judgment.

Christian love is in agreement with the norms of Christianity and can never depart from them. Genuine love is a composite of truth, justice, and holiness. Love without truth is sentimental emotionalism, while justice without love is hardness, sometimes brutality.

In reality love is a composite of all the conditions and attributes necessary for effecting psychic and spiritual contact with our fellow men. "Abide in my love" (John 15:9). By the expression "the love of Christ" is meant not primarily our love for Christ, but his love to us. This love is born within us, and grows within us, by faith in the forgiveness of our sins; without this forgiveness we can have no part in the love of Christ. For this reason there is an insoluble connection between love and the forgiveness of sins, a fact strikingly expressed in the words of Jesus about the woman in the house of Simon the Pharisee:

"Her sins, which are many, are forgiven, for she loved much; but he who is forgiven little, loves little" (Luke 7:47).

Openness

We cannot expect others to open up their soul life to us if we ourselves are close and reserved. Such a psychic isolation may have many causes, such as constitutional tendencies, *milieu*, adversity, sickness or other ailments, any or all of which may tempt to disappointment, bitterness, or frustration. Many yield to temptation and, withdrawing into their "shell," hide their innermost being from others. Some try to solve their problems by resorting to resignation, which, however, gives no positive solution, as resignation is static and negative, void of faith and hope and renewal.

The deepest and most serious causes of psychic occlusion

have connection with a wanting sense of personality responsibility, and thus they belong on the ethico-religious plane. The question does not primarily deal with the situation or need encountered, but with our manner of reacting to it.

Some persons' possibilities for reacting—and thereby their sense of personal responsibility—are circumscribed by inherited tendencies or by deficiencies in *milieu*. If a pastor or a psychotherapist is handicapped by such restrictions, he has indeed serious difficulties to contend with.

But even though their reaction possibilities may differ, every soul counselor or psychotherapist is definitely responsible for his personal reactions, whether they be negative or positive, as we all bear responsibility over against the eternal laws of God. In the last analysis the question is whether one is in accord with the will of God and with his plan for one's life.

What, then, is meant by an open personality?

Openness makes us humble both before God and man, as it helps us to admit our failures and also to acknowledge these to others. It has often been said that it is easier to humble oneself before God than before men; but the fact is that there is a close relationship between the two. If we rightly humble ourselves before God this acknowledgment will result in the right attitude toward our fellow men. Indeed, nothing is so painful and hard for us as to bow in true humility before God and really admit that we are sinners in his sight.

The Danish thinker Søren Kierkegaard says in his *Either-Or:* "Can any thinkable painful feeling be worse than to be in the wrong? Do we not see that men will submit to any kind of suffering rather than admit they are in the wrong?"

In the same book he deals with the paradox of "The edification of the concept that over against God we are always in the wrong," thus stressing the positive aspect of this acknowledgment: "The thought that over against God we are always in the wrong, this thought arrests doubt and quiets worry; it encourages and inspires to action."

But if truth is to edify, i.e., build up, it must primarily bring about a complete acknowledgment of our wrongdoing and sin against God.

Kierkegaard says further: "Ask yourself until you find the answer, for one may have acknowledged a thing many times and recognized it; one may have willed a thing, many times, and tried it; and yet, it is first and foremost the deep inner agitation, the indescribable emotion of the heart, which assures you that that which you have acknowledged belongs to you, that no power can take it from you. For only the truth that edifies (builds up) is truth for you."

The prerequisite for spiritual openness is willingness to lay everything open in the light of God. There was a time in the life of David when everything was shut up and barred for him; and he suffered greatly, both in body and in spirit. "When I declared not my sin, my body wasted away through my groaning all day long. For day and night thy hand was heavy upon me; my strength was dried up as by the heat of summer" (Ps. 32:3-4). That which closed his heart and robbed him of courage was his unconfessed sin; but when he acknowledged his sin and made restitution for the wrong he had done, his courage and joy of salvation returned.

In many instances much help is derived from opening one's heart to a Christian in whom one has complete confidence. David's relation with Nathan is a case in point.

When two persons lay bare their hearts to each other, thus sharing their need, confess their sins one to another and pray together, then *Jesus* is in the midst of them.

In this connection I desire to underscore the importance of private confession. "Therefore confess your sins to one another, and pray for one another, that you may be healed" (James 5:16).

Openness tears down barriers and removes the aloofness caused by closed hearts. It establishes contact by leading two persons onto the same plane. Opening up to each other reveals that they have much in common: problems, doubts, temptations, conflicts, defeats, sins; and this unites them in a new fellowship.

But the very deepest and strongest fellowship is obtained through the forgiveness of sins.

We must, however, guard against becoming sentimentally saccharine in our openness. One had better be somewhat wary in the use of such forms of address as *Dear friend, Dear brother or sister;* they may sound hollow. A certain amount of reserve belongs rightly in true openness.

Openness toward God leads to obedience to God. That which I experience in my life with God is to be used in the service of God and my fellow men. True, such obedience may prove costly, particularly in the field of humiliations; but God is able to make use also of our defeats, our struggles, our need and suffering. Ofttimes we feel more at home when hearing about the struggles and the distress of others than when told of triumphs and joy. Since no Christian is sinless, we are here on common ground.

On one occasion I came into great tribulation and anguish of soul. Old sins were looming large in my consciousness, sins which I had confessed to God and had acknowledged to men according to the admonition of the Spirit. But now they came back, accusing me and making it difficult for me to believe the forgiveness of sins. Again and again I sought refuge in God's promises in the Word, but confidence and rest had taken leave.

I did not understand the purpose of this anguish of soul until one day when I had a talk with a patient who at once began to tell me that she had lost her confidence of faith and was now in the midst of doubts and fears. Also in her case the darkness was caused by old sins—sins that she had confessed and for which she had received forgiveness. But now every assurance had vanished. Everything seemed dark and hopeless, so much so that she feared that she was spiritually dead. And she ended her story by saying:

"I don't suppose that the pastor understands what I am passing through."

At which I almost smiled, and suddenly a ray of light shone into my heart. I could only answer, "I have for several days had the same kind of experience as you have."

I have never seen another person evince such joy upon hearing of another's hardship. She exclaimed, "Is the pastor having the same trouble as I? I never knew that *pastors* could be thus afflicted!"

As a result we opened our hearts to one another and shared our difficulties. And even as fainthearted as we both had been, even so emboldened and grateful we became after our talk and our praying together. We were both of us able anew to appropriate to our hearts the word and promise of God.

Prayer

Earlier in this book (p. 47) we have mentioned prayer as one of the characteristic means of soul care. Now we wish to stress the importance of prayer for obtaining contact as a prerequisite in soul care.

There may be many deep-seated reactions in our personality which prevent us from getting contact with another person. There may be experiences and emotions difficult to express in words and still harder to talk about to others, as for instance: a feeling of guilt, disappointment, despondency, bitterness, mistakes, and sin.

In this difficulty prayer may be of particular help, as in prayer our deepest needs are expressed. While praying we may get release from that within our soul life with which we otherwise are loaded down. The words used are not of primary importance. Without words, but through "groanings which can not be uttered" we may pour out our inmost, deepest need to God. "To pray is to speak artlessly to God in one's heart" (Pontoppidan).

And God, who hears and answers prayer, understands us. In reality he is the only one who understands us thoroughly. In Jesus Christ God has made it manifest that he understands us, accepts us, and loves us even as we are.

As earlier stated, contact is a bipartite affair. If contact is not effected the reason may be that the one party lacks the ability to establish contact. Even in such a situation prayer is a decided help, since that which we lack may be obtained through prayer. The Word of God says, "You do not have, because you do not ask" (James 4:2).

We hear it said by way of excuse, "I am not so constituted that God can use me in that way; I have not the gift of getting in contact with my fellow men." Then it is time to ask oneself if one really has asked God to create that ability within one. "If any of you lacks wisdom, let him ask God who gives to all men generously and without reproaching, and it will be given him" (James 1:5).

But often it proves impossible for a soul counselor to establish contact. Some people are actively opposed to Christianity and make this directly evident; others are indifferent and disinterested. Having one's offer of help refused is, indeed, a painful, frustrating experience.

But even if such persons can prevent our giving them the Gospel they can not stop us from praying for them. And the experience of Christians has long since proved that *ofttimes it is more important to speak to God about a person than to speak to him about God.* In the event of stubborn frustration there is an insistent call for intercessory prayer. And prayer opens doors that are closed, and makes the impossible possible.

Love expressed in intercession creates an invisible contact which later may be a point of contact for the giving of soul care. This is so because through prayer we do, after all, get into contact with him whom we pray for regardless of time and place and spiritual state. God himself creates the contact asked for in prayer.

Through prayer we learn to know our impotence and the omnipotence of God. He wants to work his own works, but graciously allows us to be his instruments, his servants and co-laborers. Jesus has thus expressed it: "For apart from me you can do nothing" (John 15:5). While we pray he supplies his own power, thus accomplishing his work. "Whatsoever you ask in my name, I will do it, that the Father may be glorified in the Son" (John 14:13).

Often we count more on *our* work than on that of *God,* a circumstance made apparent by the manner in which we sometimes speak of prayer: "Now I have tried everything, but in vain; hence, nothing is left me but to pray." This means that prayer is a last resort when our own efforts have failed, while the Bible exhorts unto prayer *"first* of all." Prayer is, in very deed, our most important occupation.

We must, too, guard against running ahead of God, as it were, in our thoughts, ideas, plans, methods, and acts. In the right kind of prayer, offered in humility, God must be accorded first place, while ours is second. Then God will remove barriers, open closed doors, prepare ways, and bring about the contacts necessary for the gospel to accomplish its work of salvation.

Distance and Intimacy

The contact relation of soul care has a peculiar aspect all its own, "as there is something in us which requires a man at a greater distance from us and yet at the same time with a more special understanding of us than any of the personal relations earlier mentioned are in possession of." (Berggrav in his *Humor and Seriousness,* p. 79.)

This peculiar and inexplicable relation appears in the tension between distance and intimacy. If distance gets to be too dominant it generally neutralizes intimacy to such a degree that a fair exchange of thoughts is impossible. I once heard a preacher discourse on Luke 5, the section which relates the incident of Jesus' speaking while seated in Simon Peter's boat. The preacher visualized Simon also in the boat, resting on the oars, watching out that the boat did not drift so far from the shore that the words of Jesus could no longer be heard.

Some kind of distance regulator is needed for an effective interflow of ideas in soul care.

On the other hand, if there is intimacy without distance, the result will be that a contact that is to bring release and salvation will be hindered. The absence of proper distance creates such bindings as will rob the other party of initiative and of personal responsibility. The possibilities for self-development and release of personality will thus become dangerously small for the other party. How, then, may tension between distance and intimacy be safely regulated?

This is not done primarily through outward devices and methods, although these have a certain value. In the Roman Catholic soul care a kind of distance regulator is found in the structure of the confession box: a lattice between the father confessor and the penitent.

But the most important regulator is found in the personalities of the two concerned; it works more effectively than any outward device or method.

The tension between distance and intimacy depends particularly on the relation existing between one's respect for soul shyness and the personal openness required. The soul counselor should be willing to be open and at the same time show sincere respect for the innermost privacy of the person dealt with. For this, care and tact are needed, as well as intuitiveness and fellow feeling. Often silence is more essential than speech, listening preferable to questioning. But most important of all it is that both silence and speech, listening and inquiry, are used at the right time, in God's moment. But this discernment is not native with us, nor is it acquired through human precept and example. It is the gift of God, through his Holy Spirit. The decisive element is the spirit activating us.

Risks of Pastoral Care Contact

Every personal contact gives rise to a relationship of dependence, and the stronger the dependence grows the greater is the risk involved in the contact, as emotional factors then come into play. In some cases the emotional pressure may be so intense as to make control of it difficult. The established contact may release some of the most deep-seated and most repressed forces in one's psychic life; forces unsuspected by the persons concerned, both good and bad, may rise into consciousness. These emotions often oscillate between the most diverse positive and negative reactions, from warm affection and fervent love to severe disappointment, aggression, bitterness, and intense hatred.

In many transferential situations erotic and sexual emotions give rise to great difficulties. Such an affective contact causes severe temptations for both parties.

This intimate contact relation presents an ever-present challenge to the personality of pastor and psychotherapist, of whom then is required scrupulous honesty, as well as genuine humility. A soul counselor must, above all, be willing to enter into the same conflict which he wishes his fellow men to engage in. Liberation and renewal of one's own personality are prerequisites for a positive and dynamic solution of such transferential situations.

When Should Contact Be Broken?

In some cases contact effected for the purpose of soul care may have to be prolonged. Such a more or less permanent contact will, as just mentioned, often have to face various difficulties, but it will also be productive of gratifying results. The dependence relationship will gradually become an organic part of a totality, and result in much blessing as a realization and fulfilment of the word of Scripture: "Bear one another's burdens, and so fulfil the law of Christ" (Gal. 6:2).

But, apart from such special instances, soul care contact will, as a rule, be of limited duration, sometimes rather brief. Such contact is established for the time being, normally to be discontinued, as *it is superfluous when it has served its purpose.*

The question then arises: *When* is contact to be broken or dissolved? Here it is difficult to give general rules. Every case must be treated separately. But one thing is sure: Here is need of much love, decision, wisdom, and above all prayer, much prayer.

Some situations are quickly disposed of, as for instance with persons who are in the habit of consulting one soul counselor after another, since they really do not seek to find the will of God in a definite need, but to find satisfaction in the contact itself.

Samuel Keller, in his *Sonnige Seelsorge* (Sunny Soul Care), tells of a woman who sought him out and told the following story:

"I was converted many years ago. Since then I have sought guidance from all the divines in my vicinity, opening my heart to each one."—Here she named a number of clergymen.—"But none has been able to lift the veil which beclouds my soul life; none has delivered me from the fetters which bind me. But in *you* I have complete confidence."

Here the pastor interrupted her: "But I have not the confidence in myself that I may be able to do that which other servants of God have been unable to do. I will therefore suggest that we terminate this entertainment, especially as thirty inquirers who have not consulted other counselors are waiting without."

So saying, he arose.

Indignant now she, too, arose and said, "I am deeply disappointed in you. I thought that such a difficult situation as mine would be an especially interesting case for you to deal with."

"But I am not called to deal with interesting cases, nor to participate in religious entertainment, but to be of help to people in real need. You do not lack knowledge, but it remains for you to *do* that which the Spirit of God already has told you in your conscience to do. Then you will experience that 'the way of the Lord is strength to the upright.'"

She seemed struck, standing a moment with head bowed; then, collecting herself, she said quietly and with apparent meekness:

"But are we not to pray together? All the other pastors have prayed with me before my leaving."

"No; for it is written, 'If two of you *agree* on earth about anything they ask'; but we two do not agree. You want something else than I do. You want to make use of an interview with me in order to be able to say: I have had prayer communion with Pastor Keller, too. But prayer is too holy and exalted a thing for such use."

Now her eyes gleamed with anger. Without leave-taking she approached the door, but tarried there a moment and said sharply:

"Now I am convinced of the truth of that which N. N. said before my seeing you: 'I must earnestly caution the brethren against Pastor Keller, as he is not truly converted."

She let the door shut behind her with a bang, showing how insulted she felt at the rebuff.

When soul care contact is broken the main purpose should be to teach the necessity of *being alone with God*. A child does not learn to walk until he dares to let go of support. A contact broken off may become the means of liberation from dependence on man and of complete surrender to God.

But the breaking off of contact does not depend only on the one seeking guidance. The action may be equally important for the counselor, as such situations always constitute a personal challenge to him. It becomes an occasion for self-examination on his part. It is often right and wholesome for him to ask himself: Are there inhibitions and bindings, e.g., unconfessed sins, in my life? For, if such there be, they bind and inhibit the person whom he is seeking to help.

The experience of Christians shows that only to the extent in which we are set free in Christ may we be used by God to lead others to him and to help them into the same freedom.

Objectives of Pastoral Care Contact

The field of activity from which contact, as a figure of speech, is loaned tells us that soul contact as such is not the decisive element, but that the current of power which it transfers. In and by itself contact is not so important; it is only through its functional service that it becomes an effective means of accomplishment.

It is even so with personal soul care contact. It is a means for obtaining a definite objective. Contact as such has no greater value than that it becomes superfluous when it has reached its goal.

It may be likened to scaffolding, which must be constructed to make the erection of a building possible. The scaffolding is necessary for the building process and for its completion; but when the building is finished the scaffolding has served its purpose and is torn down.

The woman of Samaria became a contact-establishing person after her epoch-making meeting with Jesus. She re-entered her city and bore witness to its people: "Come, see a man who told me all that I ever did." Before, few if any would have listened to her; most likely they shunned and despised her for her loose life. But now they paid attention to her testimony and believed. Thus she became an instrument unto awakening and conversion for many, according to Scripture: "Many Samaritans from that city believed in him because of the woman's testimony, 'He told me all that I ever did'" (John 4:39). The contact which she thus effected led to the coming of many to Jesus and to belief in him; it resulted in their personal contact with Jesus. When she had done her service they were no longer in need of her witness. "They said to the woman, 'It is no longer because of your words that we believe, for we have heard for ourselves, and we know that this is indeed the Savior of the world'" (John 4:42).

Thus, the objective of soul care contact is to lead the individual to Christ by giving him the Word of God.

Personal soul care contributes toward removing hindrances in the way of the direct working of the words of Jesus. No one else than he could by his word raise up Lazarus from the dead (John 11), but to those standing by he gave the commission, "Take away the stone"; and when he, and he alone, had called Lazarus out of the grave, he gave the bystanders another task, "Unbind him, and let him go."

The task of personal soul care is to take away the stones

obstructing the road, and also to help in undoing the bindings of fettered souls.

But if soul contact is to accomplish this there must be mutual correspondence. The bridge constructed between counselor and confider must be kept open for access *both* ways. For this reason personal contact aims at *cooperation*— a cooperation built on mutual dependence and joint responsibility. The one is dependent on the help and salvation to be brought him; the other is responsible for transmitting this help rightly and effectively. Much depends here on the spirit in which this is done. If love is lacking his words are of no avail. (See 1 Cor. 13:3.) The glad tidings fail to reach their destination.

But the responsibility does not belong exclusively to the counselor. Also he who is counseled has his share. He must be willing to *admit* the truth about himself, to acknowledge it. Only then is he ready to receive the help and salvation which he needs.

The rich young ruler who according to Mark 10:17-22 came to Christ for advice was made clearly aware of what hindered him from inheriting eternal life. His contact with Jesus brought this forth. "You lack one thing; go, sell what you have, and give to the poor, and you will have a treasure in heaven; and come, follow me." But he was not willing to act on the words of Jesus; instead he went away.

The Samaritan woman, on the other hand, when her sin was pointed out to her by Jesus, acknowledged it at once; thus she was brought into fellowship with Christ, resulting in a complete change in her manner of life.

It would appear from John 19:39 that the bluntly stated truth heard by Nicodemus when he came to Jesus by night was eventually acknowledged by him, and that it led to a witnessing faith on his part.

It is therefore seen that the effect of the Word depends on whether it is received in faith. "For good news came to us just as to them; but the message which they heard did not benefit them, because it did not meet with faith in the hearers" (Heb. 4:2)

It is thus made clear that both he who seeks to help and he who is to receive the help are totally dependent on Jesus Christ, and that soul care contact is meant to effectuate this dependence. In this way a harmony of forces is created and an interaction between is made effective. And in this way is built a channel through which the power and grace of God may freely flow.

Bibliography

English:

Allport, Gordon W., *The Individual and His Religion*, New York: The Macmillan Company, 1950.

Belgum, David, *Clinical Training for Pastoral Care*, Philadelphia: The Westminster Press, 1956.

Belgum, David, *Why Did It Happen to Me? Christian Answers to Questions About Faith and Health*, Minneapolis: Augsburg Publishing House, 1960.

Bergsten, Göte, *Pastoral Psychology, A Study in the Care of Souls*, New York: The Macmillan Company, 1951.

Cabot, R. D., and Dicks, R. L., *The Art of Ministering to the Sick*, New York: The Macmillan Company, 1936.

Dicks, Russell L., *Toward Health and Wholeness*, New York, Macmillan Company, 1960.

Doniger, Simon (editor), *Healing: Human and Divine*, New York: Association Press, 1957.

Heuch, Johan Christian, *Pastoral Care of the Sick* (translated from the Norwegian by J. Melvin Moe), Minneapolis: Augsburg Publishing House, 1949.

Hiltner, Seward, *Pastoral Counseling*, Nashville: Abingdon Press, 1949.

Hulme, William E., *How to Start Counseling*, Nashville: Abingdon Press, 1955.

Johnson, Paul E., *Psychology of Pastoral Care*. Nashville: Abingdon Press, 1953.

Maeder, A., *Ways to Psychic Health* (translated from the German by Theodore Lit), New York: Charles Scribner's Sons, 1953.

143

McNeill, John T., *A History of the Cure of Souls,* New York: Harper and Brothers, 1951.

Oates, Wayne E., *Religious Factors in Mental Illness,* New York: Association Press, 1955.

Oates, Wayne E., *The Bible in Pastoral Care,* Philadelphia: The Westminster Press, 1953.

Tournier, Paul, *A Doctor's Casebook in the Light of the Bible,* New York: Harper and Brothers, 1960.

Young, Richard K. and Meiburg, Albert L., *Spiritual Therapy, How the Physician, Psychiatrist and Minister Collaborate in Healing,* New York: Harper and Brothers, 1960.

German:

Loehe, Wilhelm, *Der evangelische Geistliche,* Vol. I and II.

Harms, Claus, *Pastoraltheologie.*

Köstlin, H. A., *Die Lehre von der Seelsorge.*

Asmussen, H., *Die Seelsorge.*

Haendler, Otto, *Grundriss der Praktischen Theologie.*

Fichtner, Horst, *Theorie und Praxis der Evangelischen Krankenseelsorge.*

Thurneysen, Edvard, *Die Lehre von der Seelsorge.*

Swedish:

Engström, L. M., *Lokalförsamlingen.*

Törnvall, Gustaf, *Själavård Förr och Nu.*

Danish:

Nøjgaard, Niels, *Hvad Luther mente om sjælesorg.*

Norwegian:

Skagestad, G., *Pastorallære.*

Fjellbu, Arne, *Sjelesorg*

Nilsen, E. Anker, *Nye veier i Sjelesorgen.*